I Want My CCW

Guidebook to Concealed Weapons
An Approach from 55 Years of Law Enforcement

John Daniels

Kendall Hunt publishing company

Photo Credits:

Photos courtesy of John Daniels - pages 1 (bottom), 3, 5-6, 9, 11-12, 14-19, 21, 38, 44-45, 49-50, 61-62, 64-65, 67, 82, 91, 94, 100, 150, and 153.

Photos courtesy of Heather Daniels - pages 1 (top), 13 and 116.

Photos courtesy of Linda Daniels - pages 104, 109, 139, 146 and 149.

Photos courtesy of Eric Daniels - pages 23-26, 86, and 118.

Photo courtesy of Michael Wise - page 138.

Cover photos courtesy of John Daniels.

Disclaimer: It is your responsibility to obey all applicable local, state, federal, and international laws in the regard to the possession and use of firearms.

Kendall Hunt
publishing company

www.kendallhunt.com
Send all inquiries to:
4050 Westmark Drive
Dubuque, IA 52004-1840

Copyright © 2017 by Kendall Hunt Publishing Company

ISBN: 978-1-5249-4421-6

Published in the United States of America

Contents

This book is dedicated to you, the reader.
Thank you for choosing to carry even more responsibly by further enhancing your knowledge and skill.

I Want My CCW is designed for our audience in all 50 states. Throughout this book you will notice that California law is often sited because the authors of this book are retired officers and a current Attorney in California. However, the concepts explained throughout this book are helpful not only in California, but also in America.

Although this book is not designed as a basic handgun class lets quickly cover the basics of safety on this page before we continue to the advanced material inside.

Gun Handling Safety

1. Always keep the gun pointed in a safe direction.
2. Always keep your finger off the trigger until ready to shoot.
3. Always keep the gun unloaded until ready to use. (Carrying it CCW is considered in use – consider it stand by mode)
4. Always assume the gun is loaded until you check yourself to verify if it is unloaded

Use and Storage Safety

1. Know your target and what is beyond
2. Be sure the gun is safe to operate
3. Know how to use the gun safely
4. Use only the correct ammunition for your gun
5. Wear eye and ear protection as appropriate
6. Never use alcohol or drugs before or while shooting
7. Store guns so they are not accessible to unauthorized persons
8. Certain types of guns and many shooting activities require additional safety precautions
   - ☐ Although John Daniels is an NRA instructor this book is not associated with the NRA, or other agencies mentioned.
   - ☐ This book and training are offered by multi-award winning DefenseSHOT.
   - ☐ Visit us at DefenseSHOT.com and IwantMyCCW.com

— Chapter 1 —

CCW HOLSTERS & BELTS
REACH, RETENTION, COMFORT

IT'S HARD TO OVERSTATE HOW IMPORTANT HOLSTERS ARE. It's also one of the most overlooked aspects of concealed carry. If I have a gun that I like in the holster that is just okay, and I have another gun that is okay but I like the holster, guess which one I'm carrying every time? It's amazing how many people put time and effort into getting their CCW, getting a gun they like, training how to use their gun well, then buying a $40 holster and sticking with it. If you don't trust your holster, or it's uncomfortable, you won't carry very often. It's that simple. So don't let a holster that you don't like short circuit everything. If you have a holster that you don't like, get another one. It's not worth buying one you don't like and then sticking with a bad choice. If you get a nice holster, carrying a gun won't seem any more cumbersome than putting your wallet and car keys in your pockets, unless you're carrying a really heavy gun.

The first thing you need to decide when selecting a holster is where you intend to carry your gun. Roughly 70% of men carry their gun in the four or five o'clock position inside the waistband (IWB) which is to say, just behind their strong side hip or over the rear pocket on the strong side. It's a fairly flat area on your body, so the grip of the gun follows the line of your back rather than pointing out away from it and printing (poking out) through your shirt. It's also off of your hipbone which is much more comfortable than carrying directly over your hipbone. Roughly 20% of men keep their holster in the appendix carry position. Appendix carry means that your holster is inside your waistband, just to the strong side of your fly. Obviously a smaller/shorter gun is going to be more comfortable than a larger gun for appendix carry. The other 10% of carry locations for men are all over the place: ankle rigs, shoulder rigs, clothing with holsters built-in, and off body carry such as day planners with built-in holsters.

The numbers for ladies are slightly different. Roughly 50% of ladies prefer appendix carry, 20% between the four and six o'clock position which is to say, anywhere from behind the hip to the small of the back. The remaining 30% are divided between off body carry in purses, bra holsters, ankle and thigh rigs, corsets and clothing with holsters built into them. One of the big differences between men carrying and women carrying is that men typically find one place to carry and will carry in that position most of the time, whereas ladies will move the gun from location to location based on the type of clothing they are wearing that day and how that clothing conceals the gun. So when it comes to holsters, ladies accessorize.

IWB VS OWB
Inside the waistband holsters versus outside the waistband holsters.

Most would assume that an outside the waistband holster is going to be more comfortable. That is not always the case. Yes, it's pressing against your body less, but you're going to bump into it with your arm a lot more often. Also, an outside the waistband holster is visible below your belt, so if you're using an outside the waistband holster you're going to need a long cover garment so that the bottom of your holster isn't playing peekaboo under your jacket or shirt. Also, the typical outside the waistband holster is not as stable as the holster inside your pants. Because of this, the gun and holster flop back-and-forth more. These factors make the IWB or inside the waistband holster a vastly more popular choice for CCW.

WHAT TO LOOK FOR ON AN INSIDE THE WAISTBAND (IWB) HOLSTER

When purchasing an inside the waistband holster, I prefer holsters with strong clips rather than loops that you need to feed a belt through. It's much quicker to put on. If it takes you much longer to put your gun holster on than it does to slip your wallet into your pocket, you probably won't carry as often because odds are you'll be in a hurry when heading out the door. Donning and doffing your gun should not be a hassle. The holster with clips also allows you to reposition easily. This is nice because even the most comfortable holster will eventually cause irritation from a pressure point against your body. Having a holster with clips allows you to slide the holster forward or backward slightly, or tilt it, which relieves the pressure point. As a general rule, you're going to pay $60 or more for a holster that has decent, slim clips that engage well and aren't going to get weak.

Inside the waistband holsters typically have either a one or two clip design. The two clip design is recently gaining in popularity. This design spreads the weight of the gun out so that it is not all pulling down on one point of your waistband or belt, but it is more of a pain to put it on or reposition it, and it takes up more space in your pants. The one clip design is preferable if you have a small or light gun. There really isn't any sense in using the two clip design for a tiny, light gun. Not only is it overkill to spread the weight, it makes the gun/holster combination bulky, which is defeating the purpose of having a small gun in the first place.

WHEN CHOOSING WHERE YOU'LL CARRY CONSIDER THESE FACTORS: REACH, RETENTION AND COMFORT.

REACH

Obviously, I want to be able to keep the gun where I can quickly access it when needed. But there's always a balance between keeping the gun concealed and being able to quickly retrieve it. For most people, inside the waistband is the right balance. It's the fastest concealed place from which to retrieve a gun. The problem is sometimes you may need deeper concealment than the waistline. If you're in an area where you're more concerned about the gun being seen than normal, or if you're worried about your kids seeing it or getting to it, or if your shirt is too tight to cover, or needs to be tucked in, you may need a deep concealment holster. Deep concealment holsters keep the entire gun below the waistband. They usually have a built-in soft thin belt attached to them. The deep concealment holster and belt are made out of soft materials and are designed to be worn outside of your underwear and inside of your pants. Usually they are used with a compact or sub-compact gun. The gun is positioned behind your fly. Getting the gun from this position doesn't take much longer than the standard inside the waistband holster, except that it is only fast if you use the thumb on your weak hand to pull your pants out away from your body so that you can get to the gun. The upsides are that no one will ever look for it there, and even if they did find it, you would be aware of it. Many people that have young kids like deep concealment because there is less likelihood of their kids finding it.

Remember to check in regularly to our DefenseSHOT website at defenseshot.com and IwantMyCCW.com for updates, reviews, and recommended holsters and CCW accessories. Many of which are available directly through our website taking all the guesswork out of it and assuring you are getting correct, quality products.

RETENTION

Retention is the holster's ability to keep the gun in it. In my opinion, a holster without retention is not a holster, it's a pocket. When I started carrying decades ago, I started off using cheap holsters with no retention. Here's what happened. I wore the gun just behind my right hip. As I sat down in the bucket seat of my car the grip of the gun rubbed against the seat bolster and pulled the gun up slightly from the holster. Since I was seated, the gun would stay on my side and it felt like it was still in place. However, when I climbed out of the car I turned around and saw my gun laying in the seat. This happened a few times. Restrooms were also more challenging. When you wear a holster without retention on your pants or belt and then release the tension of the belt, the gun flops over and falls out. The other problem is that if you don't trust your gun to stay locked into the holster, you'll be checking it constantly which draws attention to your gun. I've even seen a CCW gun clattering across the floor as a result of a holster without retention.

Following are three types of retention for holsters. Leather holsters employ the use of a thumb break. This is a strap that extends up and behind the slide of your semi-automatic, or behind the hammer on your revolver. The strap then snaps onto another piece of leather on the inboard side of the holster. The gun cannot be removed from the holster without first breaking the snap. The beauty of this design is that you break the snap as you reach for the gun. Your thumb has to cross over the top of the gun anyway and in doing so it sweeps the thumb break tab, which breaks the snap releasing the gun. So this retention is both positive and seamless when drawing the gun. Unfortunately, most holster manufactures today that use leather do not offer holsters with thumb breaks because once they put a thumb break on, the holster will only fit one gun model. The strap for the thumb brake must be the exact length to fit your gun so that the snap is tight, otherwise the snap won't break easily when you sweep your thumb across the snap tab. If they don't put a thumb break on the holster, it may work okay for several guns. So marketing wise, it makes sense for them to leave the thumb break off. That way the gun store doesn't have to have a specific holster for each gun. Leaving the thumb break off is a positive attribute for the gun store and the manufacturer, but not for the consumer.

The thumb break is my favorite holster for single action semi autos with a hammer that needs to be carried in the cocked and locked position. Single action guns have a very light trigger. I like the thumb break for these guns because the strap for the thumb break is designed to sit between the back of the slide and the cocked hammer which obstructs the hammer from falling until the strap is out of the way. This creates another form of safety. Kydex holsters often use a setscrew, which clamps the holster tight to the front edge of the trigger guard. The setscrew is adjustable so that you can decide how hard you want to have the gun stuck in the holster. This style of retention requires a sharp pull to release the gun. While not as secure as the thumb break, it is enough for most.

Kydex clamshell style holsters use the clamping force of the plastic and tight fit to retain the gun. The gun is sandwiched between the Kydex and must be pulled a certain direction to be released. There are other forms of holster retention, but most of them are bulky so they are only used in open carry style holsters. Holsters with good retention and clips are safer because you can don and doff the gun and holster as one unit. As long as the gun is locked into the holster securely, it's safer to keep the gun in the holster and remove the whole thing as one unit rather than removing the gun from the holster and then taking the holster off. When the gun is locked into a quality holster, the trigger is covered, which also offers a level of safety.

COMFORT

If it's not comfortable you won't carry it. So it's worth paying for a quality holster that is smooth against your body, spreads out the footprint of the gun against you, and supports the weight of the gun correctly without being bulky. My favorite custom all leather and Kydex hybrid holsters are available at www.IwantMyCCW.com / DefenseSHOT.com. Many with discount code "BullsEye".

In my experience, ankle rigs are often used by doctors because it allows them to carry and not have the gun noticed when they are leaning over patients. The downside of ankle holsters is that they are harder to draw from. With an ankle holster you either need to take a knee or bring your foot up toward your waist to draw. These holsters are normally worn on the inside of your ankle on your weak leg. If you're right handed then you wear the ankle holster on the inside of your left leg. This way you can drop to your right knee with your left foot out ahead of you and quickly draw. I say quickly, but it's nowhere near as quick as drawing from the waistband.

Shoulder rigs are not as fun as they looked in 1980's TV shows. Most people who buy one will wear it once or twice and then realize the tight shoulder muscles and resulting headaches aren't worth it. Not to mention, it will take a minute or more to don the whole mess and get it adjusted, and it requires that you wear a jacket or cover shirt as well as a belt. Unless you're trying to hide a huge gun, forgo the traditional shoulder rig.

If you want to carry shoulder rig style, try a compression shirt designed for guns. If you are going to carry under your arm, it's important to get your week arm way up so that you don't muzzle that arm as you draw the gun. Also, keep in mind that you will be sweeping the muzzle in an ark, which means you tend to inadvertently muzzle other things as you draw. That's why most gun ranges won't let you practice with them.

You can purchase compression shirts with "holsters" (pockets) built in under each arm. When I tried these with a .40cal compact Glock27, I found that the shirt that was comfortable was not tight enough to support the weight of the gun. Instead the gun wanted to flop away slightly so I tried the next size smaller which fixed the problem of the gun sagging, but for me it was so tight that I felt like I couldn't breathe correctly. If you carry a lighter subcompact gun like at .380 you could get away with the shirt that doesn't squeeze you so tight. Or if you're in shape the tighter shirt wont bother you. The shirts are designed to be worn in place of the T-shirt with a button up cover shirt over it. If you button the button near the top of the shirt and leave the second button down unbuttoned near your chest the shirt still lays correctly and you can whip the gun out very quickly by reaching through the cover shirt— especially if you're right handed and a man, or left-handed and a woman since men's and women's shirts button in opposite directions.

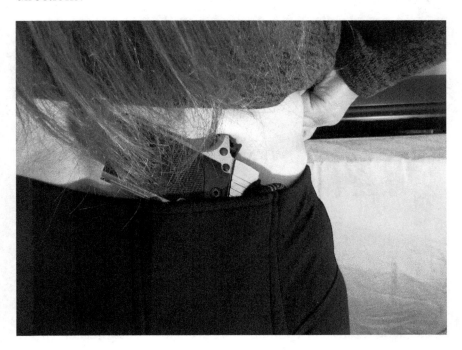

CLOTHING WITH BUILT-IN HOLSTERS

Don't put anything in the pocket that has the holster except the gun. There are many jackets and pants on the market with built-in holsters. The jackets usually have a built in holster on the inside chest pocket or the front outside pockets. Some pants with built in holsters include styles with thigh pockets that are reinforced to hold a holster and not flop around as you walk. There's even a company making yoga pants with built-in holsters. These holsters are designed to hold a small gun, like a .380. I have not tried these myself (don't picture that) but have heard positive feedback from some of my students.

CROSS DRAW HOLSTER PLACEMENT

Cross-draw means that you have your holster on your weak side usually at your waistband or under arm and are reaching across your body to get your gun. There are a few downsides to cross draw. Having your holster on your weak side and reaching across for it is going to be a slower draw than having it on your strong side. Also, ask yourself, if you were nose to nose with the assailant, which way is the gun pointed? The grip of the gun is actually pointed toward the bad guy. If he knows where the gun is he can draw your gun more easily than you can. And when he does, it's already pointed at you. Cross drawing the gun also causes you to sweep the muzzle in an ark, which is less direct and inherently less safe than strong side carry.

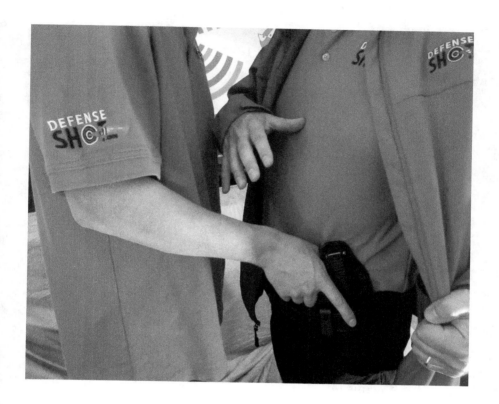

POCKET HOLSTERS

Be careful with pocket holsters. First off, if you were to carry in the pocket, it needs to be a very big, loose pocket. To see why, simply put your hand in a pocket. Now make a fist and try to pull your hand out quickly.

Also, I have seen people attempt to quickly pull a gun from their pocket only to realize it still has the holster on it when they're pointing it. The other thing you have to be careful of when having a gun in the pocket is making sure that you don't put anything else in or near that pocket. Things will not go well if you put your keys or your Chapstick in the same pocket and it ends up running around the trigger or pushing against the trigger through the cheap holster when you lean over or squat.

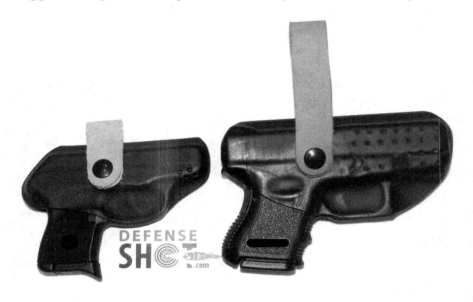

BRA HOLSTERS

Bra holsters are made of Kydex and are a clamshell design which means a single piece of Kydex molded around the gun and cut open at the bottom. To insert the gun into the holster you need to spread the clamshell far enough to get the gun started into it, and then slide it into place so that the clamshell shuts around it. These holsters have a strap that wraps from the top of the clamshell and goes around the brassiere between the cups with the holster directly beneath. To draw from this style holster, simply reach up underneath your shirt and pull down hard to release the gun from the holster. While this style wouldn't be my first choice, it does give ladies another option of where to hide the gun depending on the clothing they are wearing. It is also a form of deep concealment. So it's far less likely to be noticed and no one (kids for instance) will accidentally get access to it without her knowledge. With these clamshell style holsters, it is critical to make sure the clamshell stays tight. If the Kydex (plastic) starts to relax, the gun is more likely to fall out. Kydex is easy to heat and reshape. So if the holster becomes too loose, heating the hinge and closing the holster tightly until it cools should improve retention.

PURSES

Many ladies choose to carry their gun in a purse. In order to do this correctly, you cannot use a normal purse. The purse needs to be designed with a built in holster. Following are two basic designs for holster purses. The first is simply a purse with a holster built in as an afterthought. In order to access the gun in this type of purse, you reach through the top of the purse. This is not a good idea because it takes longer to draw, and also because you run the risk of someone seeing your gun when you're at the cash register.

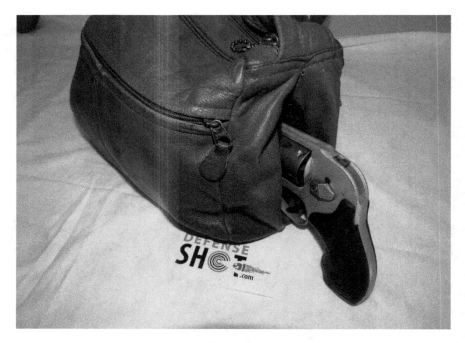

The better style of purse has a separate compartment sandwiched inside the purse with an opening on the side of the purse rather than the top. To access the gun, you open a slot in the side of the purse and reach in to grab the gun. This second style has a few advantages. First off, no one will see the gun when you're accessing the top of the purse throughout your day. Second, this type of purse allows you to point the gun at the bad guy without him realizing it. This type should be worn on your weak side shoulder. Make sure that your weak hand is grasping the strap where it meets the purse. Your hand and arm should never be placed around the purse--otherwise you will be muzzling your hand.

To access the gun, rotate your body and bring your purse around to your gun hand, this way the gun is already pointed at the attacker. Then you can slide your hand in and pull the gun loose from the holster. If you're packing a semi-automatic, you will need to pull the purse forward and rotate it away from the gun before shooting. If you try to shoot a semi-automatic from inside a purse, you are only going to get one shot because the gun is going to jam. If it's a revolver, and you are holding the purse correctly, you could shoot repeatedly right through the purse if necessary. If you do shoot the gun while it is inside the purse, it will be quieter, which is just more polite.

Most shooting facilities will not allow you to practice with a purse holster. We allow you to practice with a purse holster at our DefenseSHOT shooting facility. We will place you on the right or left end with no one behind you so that you're not sweeping anyone as you practice.

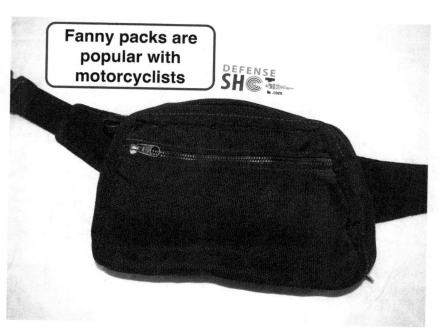

Fanny packs are popular with motorcyclists

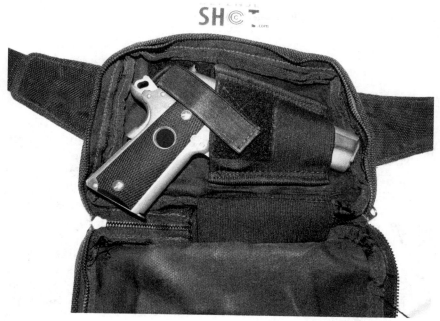

BELTS

Unless you are packing a really light, small gun on your inside the waistband (IWB) holster, you are going to want a belt. The belt will help stabilize the holster and gun so they are not flopping around. Every time pants are washed they shrink up just a little so when you put them on they are tight at the waist. Most of those tight pants become much looser over the first hour or so as you wear them. So if you put your IWB holster on without a belt and think it feels snug, don't count on it to stay snug throughout the day without a belt. The stiffer the belt is, the better it will carry the weight of the gun. I even have belts that have a super thin layer of spring steel sandwiched between two layers of leather. This allows the belt to bend laterally but not vertically. This type of belt is a great choice, especially if you're carrying a heavier gun. It distributes the weight of the gun over a larger area so that it doesn't feel like it's pulling down right at the site of the holster. Another benefit of a stiff belt is that it allows you to wear the belt one notch looser than a standard belt, without allowing the holster and gun to lose stability. Wearing the belt one notch looser is a lot more comfortable. Expect to pay around the $100 range for a quality belt.

Don't assume that every fat leather belt is a gun belt, even though they are often marketed that way. If the belt manufacturers marketing is all about how thick the leather is, there's a good chance this is not a serious CCW belt. Look for marketers who are focused on their construction and engineering. I have worn full-blown "Sam Brown" basket weave double belts on my uniform that don't afford the stability of some of the newer, thinner, and better CCW belt designs. The newer, stiffer belts are also far more comfortable than the fatter floppier belts. Another problem with the fat leather belts is that many times the clips on the holsters cannot engage correctly over the fat belt. For instance, I have one 18ounce leather belt. It's so thick that when I slide the holster behind the belt and the clips over the belt, the clips cannot close adequately enough to get a bite below the belt. As a result, when I draw the gun, the holster tries to come with it. So there is a limit to how thick or fat the belt can be before it becomes counterproductive. Good quality CCW belts are available in leather and other materials as well as a multitude of sizes, colors, widths, thicknesses, and buckle styles. Standard reversible dress belts don't make good gun belts. The buckle is usually made to be able to rotate 180°, because of this, the belt does not have much stability.

Consider not only which belt you find attractive, but also what that belt is conveying to others. For instance, if the rest of your clothing doesn't look western style, but you pick a western style belt, it's going to stand out. This could tip off observant people that you are likely carrying. The style that I refer to as "taci-cool" meaning something that looks like it belongs on a movie costume is also signaling where your gun is. Try to select something that not only matches the rest of your clothing style, but also is subdued and more discrete. If it looks like a Superhero Jr. Utility belt we know there's a gun on your waist. Companies send me thousands of dollars in equipment trying to get my endorsement, so I experience lots of products. My favorite CCW belts are available at www.IwantMyCCW.com / DefenseSHOT.com. There's a time and place for everything. Most times it's nice to give the subtle, friendly impression that you're not an easy target. This is one reason a lot of our alumni get DefenseSHOT alumni hats, shirts, and bumper stickers. I have had several alumni buy multiple DefenseSHOT alumni stickers and tell me they intend to stick them around their daughter's car. Our logo is specifically designed to look friendly, responsible and neutral, not overt. Unless you're planning on having two belts, one that is subdued and one that is not, I suggest only buying the subdued belt because there are occasions when you want to completely blend in.

When you get a new holster, test drive it inside your house for a while before taking it to the street. You'll want to make sure you're comfortable with it and have it adjusted just the way you like. Walk back-and-forth past the mirror bending and twisting to ensure it doesn't print through your clothing. Every time you get a new holster, you'll need to practice with it. First, make sure the gun is completely unloaded and then double check to make sure it's unloaded. Next, find a direction where you can point the gun safely. With your trigger finger off the gun, slowly place the unloaded gun in your holster and get comfortable drawing from it. Once you're comfortable drawing from the new holster, place your outer garment over the holster so that you can get comfortable drawing from concealment. Remember, the trick to quickly become efficient with your draw is to go slowly and exaggerate each movement. Make sure it's slow and perfect. Once you're good at that you can begin to add speed while keeping it exaggerated and perfect. Exaggerating the movements drastically accelerates the speed at which your "muscle memory" will engage. Remember, the steps are: get under the garment, grip, pull, rotate, join, extend. Joining and extending are optional, depending on how close the target is.

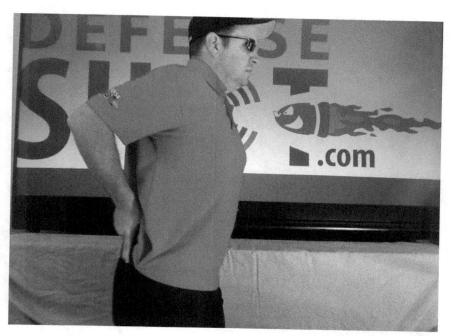

Example of
exaggerated
movements
for training

You can draw quickly using your weak hand to pull the cover garment away however it's optimal to be able to clear your garment with the same hand you are using to grab the gun. First off, it allows you to use your other hand to distract or even push the attacker away while you're drawing, and it's stealthy. When you grab the gun, you want to rake your hand in at about a 45° angle so that the web of your hand is pressed up solidly into the Beavertail of the back strap if you're using a semi-automatic. This is going to give you a much better grip on the gun. I recommend that when you pull a gun out of your holster, you bring it up as close to your armpit as possible before rotating. Not only is this going to work better in a variety of scenarios, such as in your car, but it also works better if the assailant is at point blank range. If you rotate with the gun at armpit level, you're ready to shoot into the chest area.

The old style of rotating at the hip does not work well for point blank engagement because you're going to either shoot them low which does not stop the attacker as quickly, or you are forced to point the gun up at about a 60° angle to aim at his chest, which is a terrible idea because if he bumps into you the gun is now pointed straight up at you. Remember that you never put your finger on the trigger until you have rotated the gun to the horizontal position so that it is never pointed near your leg or torso with your finger on the trigger. Your finger should not reach for the trigger until the gun is on your intended target, and you are ready to shoot. I can tell you from professional experience that under extreme stress, you'll barely be able to feel the gun in your hands, much less the pressure of your finger on the trigger. In that situation, you will be using gross motor skills only. That would not be a good time to have your finger on the trigger before you intend to shoot.

Our DefenseSHOT Defensive Shooting class is specifically designed to train you to shoot accurately and rapidly if needed, using gross motor skills only. If you've been training yourself to shoot and focus in on the pressure you feel on the trigger, or any other fine motor skills, that style of shooting will not work under pressure. People who use fine motor skills while training themselves to shoot, even if they can do so quickly and accurately, tend to spray and pray under pressure, and not put effective shots on the target. It's very important to learn how to shoot well, using gross motor skills only in our DefenseSHOT Defense Shooting class. I have repeatedly heard comments after the defense shooting class from students who just completed it saying that prior to the class they were a really good marksman, but now they realize, with the perspective of their new skills, that prior to this training, they were completely unprepared to defend themselves under pressure. Some may assume this class is going to be like having a drill sergeant screaming in their ear all the time, but nothing could be further from the truth. The class is very laid-back and fun. This class will teach you how to work under pressure because you'll be learning how to shoot using your gross motor skills, while also installing that skill set in your subconscious. In this way, the skills work regardless of your level of stress.

Our DefenseSHOT state-of-the-art use of force simulator class gives you the opportunity to safely work on your draw under pressure in a multitude of scenarios. Not only will you learn to read different situations so that you know when to draw and when not to draw, but the computer will also time your draw and trace the direction of your draw so that you can learn how to make it as direct and quick as possible. Also, since it's keeping score for you, if you have a competitive nature, you'll be able to treat the training as a game and compare your times against your buddies or yourself if you like. If you're not competitive, that's fine too. You'll be able to use the diagnostic tools to improve your abilities. Taking advantage of these classes gets you ready to defend yourself. Simply doing the minimum training to get your concealed weapons license in hand is not enough. Doing that amount would be analogous to buying a race car and then assuming that you can jump out on the track effectively and safely. The driver and his skills are far more important than the car he is driving. You could put a skilled driver in a family car and watch him drive circles around and unskilled driver in a high-performance vehicle. Skill trumps hardware.

Take the classes that will give you the skills *you* need. You don't want to be in a fair fight when your life, or the lives of other innocent people are on the line. If you are in a fair fight your tactics and skills weren't adequate. Our DefenseSHOT classes are fine-tuned to deliver you the maximum amount of training with the quickest learning curve possible. It's not an overstatement to say that our DefenseSHOT alumni who finish our defense and advance defense shooting training have a better, more complete and effective toolbox to work from than an average cop. Some of our local Sheriffs departments get excellent training, but if I were to pick a random group of cops nationwide, I could guarantee my alumni have a better skill set. Just the other day one of our alumnae who went through the defense and advance defense shooting classes in one day called me. He said after class he went home and shared with his neighbor who works for the highway patrol what he had learned that day. The officer was amazed and repeatedly told him that he wished he could get trained to that level at work. Our training is proprietary, meaning the tactics I provide are not available anywhere else. Also, the bureaucracy and red tape that hold most agencies back do not burden us. As a result, you're getting cutting edge training at the most efficient learning speed possible. As another example, we have had many students who previously completed a five-day, nationally recognized class who were not able to compete with students who had completed our three-hour defense shooting class. Time spent is not always an indication of skills acquired. So sign up for our shooting classes, have fun, learn quickly, and make sure it's not a fair fight!

— Chapter 2 —

COMMON MISCONCEPTIONS ABOUT BEING RESPONSIBLE

ONE COMMON MISCONCEPTION is that other people will take care of your self-defense. Self-defense is just that. You cannot delegate your responsibility. If you yourself are not providing your self-defense, no one is. Based on its very definition, self-defense must be done by you. You cannot rely on family members, friends, cops, or anyone else for your self-defense. No one can take care of you as well as you can. You are the only one that's always with you. No matter where you go, there you are!

Failing to prepare is preparing to fail. Some people would say they are not looking for trouble and that's great! The problem is, trouble is looking for you, and if it finds you, you need to be ready. Also, keep in mind that you do not want to be in a fair fight if your life is on the line. As the victim, you are starting at a disadvantage because the speed of initial action usually beats reaction. You need to be prepared and trained *ahead* of time to overcome this disparity. It's going to be pretty important that you are the victor here. Again, we are not playing a game of reciprocity. We are not intending to kill the person who is trying to kill us, or another innocent victim. For us, winning simply means stopping the threat. As soon as the threat stops, the gunfire stops. Usually the gunfire doesn't even start since most people don't feel bulletproof.

Another misconception is if I don't worry about it, it's not my problem. This is simply not true. It's like saying, if I cover my eyes the world isn't there. Others say "Don't get trained or you'll have more liability since you know the law." That idea is completely false. In fact, I've seen a dad prosecuted because his son used a gun for self-defense, then missed the shot and hit his dad by accident. The dad was charged with felony reckless endangerment because he instructed his son only how to load it "in case of emergency" without any official training. The prosecutor was concerned with the lack of proper training. If the son had been trained, (even if he missed) it would have been a different story. Ignorance does not exonerate people from responsibility. Often ignorance magnifies responsibility.

In every life there are rites of passage, moments that help to transform who we are. As an example some tribes have boys go off and live by themselves for a few days without any support. When he returned he had likely changed his perspective. Today, those who have children know that that moment changes you a bit. There are many rites of passage. This has to do with actions that turn on genetic memory known as epigenetics. What we think of as instinct. Rites of passage are activities or experiences that activate genetic memory or affect your instinct. There are businesses today that specialize in taking people hunting. This has become a market focusing on officials and competitive business people, many of whom have found hunting to be a rite of passage that somehow turns on more instinct. These people come to hunt because they have found it to be a rite of passage that gives them a competitive edge in business. One difference between being a man or a woman, rather than a guy or girl, is taking responsibility for ourselves. Taking on the mantle of responsibility for defending ourselves is no different.

There is a reason that CCW carriers are statistically so law abiding. Your new responsibility, this new mantle, changes you just a little. You suddenly become a more responsible person because of your new perspective. Once we are prepared to defend ourselves, then the next branch out from that is to be able and willing to defend others around us. For many, this is a better motivating factor than

PHILIPPIANS 1:21 KJV
For to me, to live is Christ, and to die is gain.

defending ourselves. For instance, some Christians are not afraid to die and are rather looking forward to it since they know where they are going next. These people aren't as interested in defending their life as they are defending the lives of others. We also have to keep in mind that Paul—the person who wrote the above Biblical quote—did not have family to provide for. Having others who depend on you changes the equation. It's kind of hard to provide for your family if you are dead.

Another common theme is; "I'm so afraid of a lawsuit that I don't want to carry a gun." How does this idea affect your family? It leaves them hanging. I have talked with mercenaries who have seen men on the side of the road so distraught they are pulling handfuls of hair out with their scalp bleeding because their family is gone and they couldn't protect them. Or the even more common, "I'm not going to get involved because I don't want to be in a lawsuit." To those people I respond, "There are worse things than a lawsuit."

We have a moral obligation to take care of those around us. Imagine if anyone you cared about was permanently injured or killed and then you found out there was somebody else on scene who could've stopped the threat? Can you imagine deciding *not* to get involved and later finding out what a great person he/she was? Imagine if you are in a room full of strangers. You may not feel much obligation to protect them. Now imagine being introduced to each of the people, their families and friends to learn their backgrounds and the things they liked. Now would you be more likely to help out? The fact that you don't know the backgrounds of everyone should not detract from their value as humans. Inaction, neglect or hostility is often justified by depersonalizing or dehumanizing the victim. We have a moral obligation to take care of those around us.

There is an important distinction between helping people you know and people you don't know. When you know the people, it's easier to tell who is good or bad since you know one of them and you've been paying more attention to what they're doing. When stepping in to help someone you don't know, take an extra second to ensure you have properly assessed the situation and are interceding on the behalf of the correct person. We don't want to get involved only to realize it's a plainclothes Officer affecting an arrest. Or another CCW person who is trying to save someone's life. You also need to be careful about getting involved in any domestic dispute where the husband is attacking his wife or vice versa. Domestic disputes are an officer's most dangerous call. Often, when we step in and separate the two, the victim attacks the officer to save the aggressor. This is known as Stockholm syndrome.

Stockholm syndrome was so named because back in 1973 there was a bank robbery in Stockholm, Sweden, where

31

the robbers took hostages for an extended period of time. The hostages began to identify with their captors, and actually worked on the attackers' behalf against the victims' own best interest. Today, Stockholm syndrome is taking entire countries under its grasp, including Sweden (but that's the subject of a different book.) In these situations, the victim suddenly identifies with and tries to help the aggressor. As a CCW carrier, you're not there to provide marriage counseling. We only get physically involved in a situation like this if someone is in imminent danger of great bodily injury or death. If these two have been doing this over and over, it may look a little more serious than it is. Maybe, he's going to give her a black eye, but not put her in the hospital. It must be the threat of serious bodily injury, a bloody nose is not serious bodily injury but getting your head slammed into the side of a table or the ground is. Anyone threatening another with any hard, pointed, or edged object that can be used as a weapon is as well.

An attack known as, "putting the boot to someone," can also cause great bodily injury, especially when the victim is down and the attacker is kicking the victim in the head or neck. The hard part is making that call if both people are standing and one is simply throwing a punch. After all, even this could occasionally amount to serious bodily injury. I have seen people get their eye socket broken in one punch. That constitutes great bodily injury. The person with the broken eye socket needed extensive surgery.

Disparity in size between the aggressor and victim, or a difference in age, disability or other physical state may factor into the likelihood of serious bodily injury from fist blows. When you decide to interject yourself into an incident with strangers, take that extra second to assess the situation and make sure you're on the right side. During this extra moment you can be quietly moving yourself to a position of advantage— a concept you will become familiar with in our, "Advanced Defense Shooting class." In case someone is about to be seriously injured or killed. This class will help you identify the threat, assess the situation and react if need be.

Some may feel if they are not trained that they are not taking on this obligation. That's not true. If the boat owner refused to

1 TIMOTHY 5:8 KJV

"But if any provide not for his own, and specially for those of his own house, he hath denied the faith, and is worse than an infidel."

buy life vests would that make him less responsible for anyone who drowned? Sure, he wouldn't have to worry about handing them out as the boat goes down but ultimately he still had a responsibility. I am not talking about what is legal versus illegal when it comes to your responsibilities. I'm talking about morality. Today we live in a society of people who will stand around and film someone getting attacked rather than stepping in. Just because that is the new norm doesn't make it right. Just because you are tried in a court or court of public opinion doesn't mean you won't be tried by your own conscience.

Making the decision to take care of yourself and others is step one. Training and being ready to defend yourself is step one. Defending others is step two. Simply dragging the gun around with you does not make you ready. That would be like owning a car and only learning to drive it in a parking lot at five miles per hour and expecting to jump onto the freeway in heavy traffic. A person who does that is going to find themselves in way over their head. This is why I highly recommend attending our intermediate defense shooting and advanced defense shooting classes. These classes are designed to get you ready. They will fill your toolbox with the different tools and experiences you will need. We start off slow with target shooting. Then we slowly transition into defensive shooting, which is a completely different skill set. Target shooting, you're able to take your time and use your conscious analytical mind to think about your sights, your trigger control, and holding the gun still. In a defensive shooting situation there will be no conscious analytical mind available. If all you have ever done is target shooting using your conscious analytical mind, you're shooting ability just went out the window as well. People who have only learned to target shoot tend to spray and pray under pressure and not hit anything.

Defense shooting teaches you new skills. It also pushes these new skills off into your right brain, (or subconscious), so that they are still available even under pressure. You're going to be able to react effectively far faster and smoother. When you learned to drive, at first you had to think consciously about what you were doing, *long skinny pedal go fast; fat pedal go slow or stop. Little stick next to the steering wheel, push down for left signal; push up for right.* Because they were in your conscious analytical mind but not yet in your subconscious, your reaction time was terrible and your driving was stuttered and jerky. If someone pulled out in front of you, you first had to think, *fat pedal go slow* before your foot moved to the correct control. Your reaction time was laughable. By contrast, when was the last time you thought about the petals or your turn signal? You don't think about any of those things because they are now in your right brain, your subconscious. What has happened to your driving ability? It became far smoother, more accurate, and your reaction time is a tiny fraction of what it was. Shooting is similar. Once you have learned these new skills and they are placed into your subconscious, you'll be able to shoot six rounds a second or more on target, and be able to shoot multiple targets; use fast effective target acquisition without needing your sights and many other important skills for defense. Learning to shoot this way will take all of your shooting skills, including your target shooting to a whole new level. It's also a whole lot of fun.

In the advanced class you will learn to use your surroundings to your advantage. How to shoot around barricades such as walls or doorways, over the hood of the car correctly, shoot from the hip accurately, and how to shoot correctly while retaining the gun and pushing the target off of you at point-blank range. The last skill mentioned is very likely to be needed. Shooting someone 21 feet away is a luxury that you often don't have. Usually the bad guy will be right up in your grill. If you've never shot this way before you can't expect to be ready to do it the first time while you're being attacked. This skill is best learned under supervision before you need to use it under pressure. You will also learn how to clear buildings. To my knowledge I am the only one around teaching at this level to non-law-enforcement. It is a valuable skill for you to have. I don't want you to go around kicking in doors and clearing buildings, but if you're already in the building, you need to know how to move around if necessary to get a phone or a loved one or get out. Having this skill set puts you on an even playing field with others who have the skill set. It will allow you to use your surroundings to your advantage far more effectively.

You'll be able to shoot effectively while moving quickly. You're only capable of doing under pressure what you have already trained to do at the shooting facility. This is why in shootings you'll often see people step out from behind the front of a truck, or other cover they could've used to their advantage, and stand out in the open shooting. They do this because it's almost impossible to do something new and different under pressure. So if you have already trained and become comfortable with it, you will be able to do it. This is why we train learning to shoot while moving, shooting around barricades, and getting experience with other skills that you'll need to know.

In the law enforcement Academies we studied, "Officer-involved shootings," in detail. One common problem we noticed was the officers who were using revolvers were found with empty brass in their pockets after a gunfight. You would think, *why in the world did this guy who was in a gunfight take the time to empty the cases out of his revolver, put them in his hand, and then place them in his pocket before reloading his gun?* Answer is: that's what he did at the range. He didn't think anything of unloading his revolver, dropping the empty cases into his hand and sticking them in his jacket pocket so he didn't have to pick them up off the ground. The problem is when you're under extreme stress, you're basically on autopilot, so whatever you have been doing at the shooting facility is what you're going to do in a fight. If all you have done is stand at the table and take your time trying to poke holes in the bull's-eye, you're not even close to ready. Everything we do at the shooting facility has a reason. When you are covering targets and pausing on each bull's-eye rather than waving the gun back-and-forth, there's a reason.

Everything has a reason, and each skill sets you up to be ready for the next skill. If you have never shot while leaning out around the barricade, that ability will not be available under pressure. If you have not learned to shoot while moving, it will be almost impossible for you to resist the urge to stop moving before taking a shot. Or you will keep moving but your shot placement won't be accurate. It's so important to learn these things ahead of time so that you own these new abilities. "The defense and advanced defense shooting classes," are offered back to back on the same day. You have the option of splitting them up if you prefer. The advanced class builds off of the skills you learned in the defense shooting class, so it's important that you take the intermediate defense shooting class first.

We're all familiar with how expensive ammunition is. It's easy to burn hundreds of dollars worth of ammo in a couple of hours. But if you do this without receiving training while you're doing it, normally there's no discernible difference in your skills. To make things worse, if you have been doing anything wrong, every shot you take is further ingraining that bad habit. Practice does not make perfect; practice makes permanent. I don't encourage people to "warm-up" at a range before coming for training. If you know how to load and unload the gun and handle it safely, which can usually be accomplished with a single trip to the range, you're better off not trying to practice on your own before coming to class. People who consider themselves beginners often progress faster and with greater accuracy and speed than those who have experience. They are a blank slate and have not picked up bad habits we have to erase before learning new skills. By taking the training classes you'll burn less ammunition while learning far, far more than you ever could simply going out and burning ammunition by yourself. Trying to train yourself how to shoot, especially if also trying to learn defensive shooting skills, or learning it by watching TV is about as effective as trying to learn karate by reading a book. Since you're burning ammunition, if you're trying to train yourself to shoot it's far more expensive than karate chopping the air would be. The training is a bargain. Please take advantage of it so you're prepared to protect yourself and others.

— Chapter 3 —

QUICK ACCESS GUN CONTAINERS AND SAFES
HELPFUL HINTS FOR QUICK ACCESS DOJ GUN STORAGE CONTAINERS & SAFES

IF A CHILD GETS A HOLD OF YOUR GUN and scares someone with it, or takes it out your front door, or injures somebody with it, you can be charged with a crime or open to a law suit. Also, in California, if your gun is in your vehicle and you leave the vehicle with the gun still inside the car, you must have the gun locked in a container that is connected to the vehicle because if someone gets in the car and takes the gun, you can be held responsible as well.

Keeping these situations in mind, I recommend getting a small California Department of Justice approved container that can be mounted to the vehicle or can be connected to the vehicle with a cable. Small DOJ approved firearms containers are available for this purpose. I recommend one that will either mount to the vehicle or you can buy a container that comes with a small cable with a loop on one end and a metal knob on the other end of the cable. It's designed to lasso around your seat post, and the small metal nub goes through a small cut in the side of the container. When the door closes on the container, the metal knob is stuck in the box locking it to the container. Now to make things confusing, there is a federal law regarding guns in the car, versus a California law having locked guns in the car.

The federal law stipulates that if you are driving the vehicle and you have a gun in the car that is not covered on your CCW, the gun must be unloaded *and* in a locked container. This law does not stipulate that the container must be a California Department of Justice approved container, but it does stipulate that it cannot be: the glove box, center console, or another container that is permanently attached to the vehicle. Because of this, if you were to hypothetically take a D.O.J. approved container and bolt or screw it to the floor panel of your vehicle, it would then *become* a permanent container that is part of the vehicle. Because of this, the container would be seen as the same as a factory center console or glove compartment which are not acceptable when transporting a firearm in any DMV approved vehicle, whether it's a car, boat, RV, motorcycle, quad... anything for which you pay DMV fees.

Now, if you were to take that same box and place it in the vehicle *without* permanently attaching it to the vehicle, then that container would be acceptable as a "locked container" while transporting a gun. The ammunition cannot be in the container with the firearm, and it cannot be touching or next to the container where the gun is locked. The gun and ammo *must* be on opposite ends of the vehicle for the purposes of transporting the firearm. To restate: federal law mandates that any firearm not listed on your CCW (for those states where your guns are listed) must be properly secured according to this protocol.

Here's where it gets interesting: California has just (2017) passed a new law that states if you walk away from the vehicle and the gun is left inside the vehicle, then the gun must be locked in a container that *is* connected to the vehicle. So in this case, the container can be bolted, screwed or welded to the vehicle; however, if you permanently connect the box to the vehicle by bolting or welding it, that box would no longer be legal to transport the gun if the gun is not on your CCW. However, if you take that same box and simply connect it to the vehicle with a cable or cables, then the box would still be acceptable as a box or container that can be used to transport firearms in the vehicle that are not listed on your CCW, confused yet? If the box is permanently mounted to the vehicle, then it is considered part of the vehicle, like the glove box or center console, which are areas where you are *not* allowed to transport a gun that is not on your CCW. If you want to have a box that you can use for CCW guns and for transporting guns not listed on your CCW, chose the cable lock. If you only want the box for CCW guns, feel free to permanently mount it to the vehicle. To clarify, your CCW gun does not need to be locked up while you are transporting it as long as it is under your direct control.

With the new California law, if you were to leave the gun in your vehicle while you're not in the vehicle, then the gun needs to be in a locked container that is connected to the vehicle either by a cable lock or otherwise connected to the vehicle, so in this case if you had wanted to place a dedicated box in your vehicle specifically for holding your CCW gun in California, when the car is not under your direct supervision, then in this case the box could be welded, screwed or bolted to the vehicle and in this case be part of the vehicle for the purposes of leaving the gun in the box while the car is not under your direct supervision. This new law comes as a result of hundreds of firearms being stolen out of police vehicles in Southern California because currently people down there were just taking the guns and tossing them in the trunk of their car while walking away. Other people were seeing this happen and realizing they could get a free gun out of the trunk of the car or glove box. As a result, a law was passed stating that the guns must be secured if you walk away from the vehicle.

Many "gun safes" are available for this purpose. I say gun safes in quotes because I don't consider these to be safes; they are gun containers. They'll keep the honest people out, but anyone with some basic tools could easily break into them. Because of this, I recommend these boxes be kept out of sight in the vehicle so that they do not become a temptation to passers by.

Many will elect to put a lock box inside the center console of their vehicle this is especially easy on many trucks that have a center console directly above the floor pan. Many cars are built the same way. There are several designs, and name brands available of small California Department of Justice approved containers that will fit inside a center console or under the driver's seat.

One very common container is the **Gun Vault Nano**. It's about the size of a Bible. It's available with or without a biometric lock. In this case, the Gun Vault Nano has four gray buttons on the top that line up with your fingers. You program the container with a specific sequence of button push. The box has a hand shaped cutout that lines your fingers up with buttons. This feature is more convenient because you don't have to fumble around for keys and retails for around $100. Other brand names are available if you decide to use a biometric lock box. I recommend only getting biometric (fingerprint) locks if they have a redundant set of buttons to back up that lock so that you have a secondary way of opening them. The fingerprint biometric locks don't tend to be foolproof and they especially don't like to work when you're trying to use them quickly. Also, in a high stress moment, your fingers will begin to sweat. When this happens, don't even try to use the biometric. It most likely won't work.

Remember, the gun that is least likely to be stolen is the one that no one knows exists. Keep a low profile when placing your gun into the container. Make sure no one is near the vehicle that can see what you're doing as you place the gun into the container. Ideally, you want a container that is large enough to allow you to place the gun in the box while it's still in its holster since unholstering the gun takes away one of the safety measures. It's safer to slide the entire holster off and place it in the lock box than it is to unholster the gun and place it in the box by itself.

Keep in mind that the only time the gun is locked in the box, if it's your CCW gun, is while it is *not* under your direct supervision. This box needs to be connected to the vehicle, but the law does not stipulate that it needs to be bolted, screwed or welded to the vehicle, so you could take that same container and simply connect it to the vehicle by way of cables or a single cable. This is nice because if the box is connected by cables, it is not considered part of the vehicle. So if you wanted to transport a gun in your vehicle that is not listed on your CCW, this box could do double duty for that purpose since it is not considered part of the vehicle if it is cabled to the vehicle. This box, when cabled to the vehicle, could be used to transport guns that are not on your CCW when they are unloaded with the ammunition in a separate part of the vehicle.

If you have a gun, but it is not under direct supervision, and a kid gets a hold of it, you can be in trouble for that. If you ever have kids in your home and have a gun in the home, the gun needs to be locked in a California Department of Justice approved container when it's not under your direct supervision. Next, we'll go over some tips for using or selecting these California Department of Justice approved containers.

MOUNT CONTAINERS

Mount Containers are intended to be stationary to the floor or heavy furniture. This will keep the honest people from walking away with your gun container. It will also help to keep a kid from picking up the box and shaking it when there may be a gun inside.

Memorize any codes, write them down and keep them with the key. Most of these boxes, even if they are biometric or open

41

with buttons will also have a backup key in case the battery dies. Make sure that you keep this key in a place that is not obvious, and where it cannot be found by kids. When it comes to a code, it's much easier to pick a code that means something to you, so that you're less likely to *need* to write it down, but make sure it's nothing too obvious like a birth date, your address, or too obscure. If you use multiple small containers, use the same code on them all so that you don't get confused as to which container has which code.

Periodically, check safes with electronic locks to verify their battery power. I've done tests on batteries with several of these lock containers. The Duracell batteries last well over a year for most people with regular use; however, since it is a safety issue, I recommend changing the Duracell battery once every six months. Additionally, there are push button code California Department of Justice approved containers that do not need batteries; however; they tend to be bulkier.

BIOMETRIC

Should you choose Biometric, practice opening your biometric locks on a regular basis to ensure competency. Biometric locks are handy, but I wouldn't trust my life to them. For years, on and off duty, I found that a struggle is likely if I am in a hurry. They don't tend to work well if your hands are dirty or sweaty. Obviously, this could be a problem in a stressful situation. As a result, I only recommend a biometric safe if there is a push button backup also readily available on the same box.

SMALL, KEY-LOCK, BOOK-STYLE CONTAINERS

This variety is best used for complying with regulations, not preventing access. These little gun boxes are not Fort Knox. They're not going to keep someone out who intends to gain access. On several occasions, I have had people bring these boxes to our shooting facility and hand them to me explaining that they left the key at home, or could not get the box open... Usually, I'm able to get into these boxes within a couple of minutes with a pair of needle nose pliers, a screwdriver, or a small punch. Most of these boxes have an exposed piano hinge on the back side of the door, and if you punch it with a hammer, you can drive the wire out of the hinge and open the box from the hinge side without causing damage to the container.

DOCUMENT CONTAINERS

I have also had people bring firearms in document containers to my classes and asked me to take their gun out of the box because they had forgotten the key or code. Usually, I could go on YouTube and punch in the name of the container and watch a teenager showing me how to get into the box with a screwdriver, paper clip or other similar easily found items. Many times I've been able to get into these containers in a matter of seconds. These boxes are to keep the honest people out so to speak, or to keep people from getting at them in a hurry. This is another reason that this container should not be in plain sight. Remember, the most secure gun is the one that is in a secure location that no one knows exists.

Select a gun container based on how it opens and where you want to place it. Before purchasing the container, think about where it will be placed and where you'll be able to get at the controls for the box. For instance, if you want the gun to be placed in the center console of your vehicle you won't want to pick a box that has buttons that you can't easily see or reach when it's in the console. Also, consider where the hinges are on the box. You don't want to bring the box home and realize that it can't be opened once mounted in the center console because of the way the door needs to swing.

For long-term storage, consider larger more sturdy gun safes that are not easy to pry open. The smaller boxes are used simply for the gun (or guns) that you need to be able to get to at a moment's notice, not for your long-term storage. Guns such as your "Safe Queens" that only go out to the range once a year.

Select a container at least large enough for your handgun obviously, but it would also be nice to have the box large enough to accommodate the gun while it is still inside your CCW holster. Keep in mind these boxes are lined with foam. Foam is nice if the gun is out of the box because it keeps it from getting scratched by the interior metal of the box; however, if the gun is in its holster, the foam inside the box may not be necessary which would afford you more room inside the container for the gun inside of its holster.

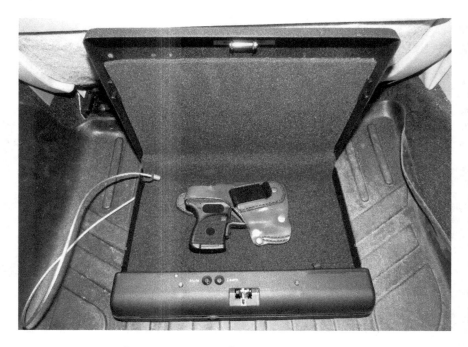

You get what you pay for—select the most expensive container that meets your needs. I have a lot of experience with varying brands and styles of these boxes. Typically the cheaper ones don't work as well as you might expect. They also tend to be less secure. I am personally less apt to spend money on a biometric lock but I *am* willing to pay more for a box that is built more substantially. Typically the containers that are made by companies that also make tool boxes are more cheaply made or are designed in a way that doesn't function as well. The gun boxes that tend to work better are the ones from companies that specifically make gun boxes as opposed to the companies that seem to do them on the side as an afterthought.

CONTAINER PLACEMENT IN CASE OF HOME INVASION

The people who get their homes invaded the most are drug labs, and we can learn something from these guys. Whenever you go into the drug lab, or a home full of drugs, you can expect to find a gun in the couch cushion or next to the seat near the TV. Why? Because that's where most people spend their time, parked in front of the TV. If someone kicks in your door you're not going to have time to run to the bedroom, so it's a good idea to have something close by. Now, don't get me wrong, I do not want you to stuff a gun in your couch cushion or start a drug lab, but if you can find a place near your chair where you can place a quick access safe, that's a good idea.

GUN SAFES

Use price point as an indicator of quality. As a general rule, the decent quality safes start in the neighborhood of $500 and go up from there, depending on size and extra amenities. This is a purchase that is going to last you a lifetime, so it doesn't make sense to skimp.

Please, do not buy a thin metal $150 box with two key locks on the front of the door; this is not a safe, all you're doing by getting one of these is placing all of your valuables in one convenient place for the burglar. My uncle Steve who was also a Deputy used this to his advantage. He bought a $50 "safe" and put some cheap costume jewelry in it, and then he hid his valuables elsewhere. When the house was burglarized, the dummy took the worthless costume jewelry and assumed he had cleared the place of its valuables. He never found the good stuff.

When shopping for gun safes, the price is usually a good indicator of quality; however, you can buy the same quality box at varying prices depending on where you purchase the safe. For instance, I've noticed that if you buy the safe at a store that specifically only sell safes, or at a gun store, they tend to be more expensive than if you bought it at a big box store or an online retailer. Often these big box stores will deliver the safe to your home for free with curbside service, meaning that they will roll the pallet into your garage or first floor as long as the pallet jack will role there. If you need it moved inside your home, they are also typically cheaper than the gun stores with "white glove service", which is what they call it when they have to carry the safe into your home.

Some of the larger Cadillac type safes such as the $2000 and $3000 Canon safes offer installation by a team that will purposefully travel significant distances to reach their customers. In the case of Sacramento, it's not unusual to have an installation crew from the Los Angeles area. This means that, yes, they know where it is, but they are a lot less likely to make a one-day drive to swing by and see what's inside your safe.

Many safes are designed so the door can be removed from the front of the safe when moving. This cuts the weight of the safe in two halves. Separating them makes it much easier to move upstairs, so if you're planning on putting a safe upstairs, you might want to make a note of which models have doors that are removable. This does not make the safe inferior to models without removable doors since the doors are only removable after the door has been unlocked.

PLACING THE SAFE

The best location for your gun safe is where no one will ever see it or suspect its whereabouts. You don't want to place the safe in an area where workers coming to service your appliances will notice the safe as they wander through your house. Often burglars are people that have been in your house in the recent past. They tend to case the joint, and then come back when the opportunity arrives. I can recommend local, trustworthy contractors (who also have CCWs) who can install gun safes in your home and will even build a pseudo wall, cabinet, or stairs in front of the safe so that no one will ever suspect it. Often, if you look around homes closely enough, you'll notice little cubbyholes or other dead space areas where you could place a safe and build an obstruction in front of the safe.

If you're planning on putting the safe in your garage, I highly recommend putting something in front of it so that passersby don't see it as they drive by when your garage door is left open. Often, people will put a black shower curtain in front of the safe, or other obstruction, that can be easily moved aside for access. I also recommend concealing the name brand on the door of your safe if it's in a place where anyone will ever see it. If someone notices that you have XYZ brand safe, they can go online and find out the shortcomings of that specific brand of safe, which makes it more easily cracked if they decide to attack it at a later date. Many videos on YouTube show you how to crack into certain name brand safes. Interestingly, these videos are often made by a competing gun safe company, trying to demonstrate their product's superiority; the directions for burglarizing is an unintended consequence of economic competition.

For added security, consider bolting the safe to the floor. Many safes have pre-drilled holes in the floor for this purpose. One of the easiest and most common ways to break into a safe is to knock it over and cut through the floor of the safe with a cutting blade. Even if a thief chooses not to cut through the floor of the safe, knocking it over makes it much easier to pry open the door than if the safe were standing upright. It doesn't matter if the door is a foot thick if the box around it is 16 gauge steel it will still be easy to pry away from the door with 6-foot bars if the safe is on its back. Keep in mind that no matter how thick the door is, or how many bolts are on it, the box of the safe is typically the same on most safes- it's just a metal box. Picking the lock is the least likely plan of attack, as a general rule, they will attack the box itself. Not bolting it to the floor makes that easier.

When bolting your safe to the ground, a concrete floor is most secure. During installation, use a concrete drill to drill holes into the concrete and place red head bolts (self-expanding bolts) into the concrete. These bolts are placed through the holes in the bottom of the safe itself, and when tightened down they expand into the concrete. If you can't place it on concrete, consider using large bolts that go completely through your hardwood floor with large backup washers or a metal plate underneath the floor that is then bolted on and tack welded. If you're unable to bolt the safe to the floor at all, consider placing it in a very cramped area where a burglar won't have the ability to easily move it and tip it over on its back.

Keep in mind that the safe is going to weigh a lot more once it's filled. A 700-pound safe once filled with guns, ammunition and other goodies can easily double and weight, and in this case, weight is your friend. It's not unusual for a new large safe to weigh 1100 pounds before you put anything in it.

THE PUNCH TEST
The way that safes lock their door is by pushing large metal bolts out to the sides and often also the top and bottom to lock into the metal box they're attached to. Some of the cheaper safes can be "punched" meaning that if someone were to drill a small hole through the side of the safe and put a small metal rod through that hole, lining it up with one of these large bolts and then simply push on the rod, it will push the safe bolt back into the door, and the door opens right up. Most of the better safes have figured that out and are punch proof. It's very easy to see if the safe you are about to buy is punch proof. Simply open the safe door and engage the locking mechanism with the locking bolts in the extended position. If the safe is punch proof, you will *not* be able to push the bolts/lugs back into their retracted position in the safe door. If the bolts push back in by hand while locked, the safe is not punch proof.

FIRE RATINGS
Fire ratings are important. If the gun safe is rated for thirty minutes that might be enough time to keep everything inside

from turning to ash, but it's probably not enough to keep everything inside from being destroyed or turned dark brown. Thirty-minute gun safe fire ratings are very common in entry price range safes. They're better than nothing, but I recommend springing for a safe with a one-hour plus rating. This is especially important if you live in a rural area since it's more likely to take longer for the fire to be put out, or if you need to place the safe on an interior wall of your home, because the interior walls of your home are going to get a lot hotter in a fire than an exterior wall. The price tends to go up fairly dramatically as the fire rating increases, and really all they're doing to increase the fire rating is adding more gypsum board inside the safe, which is really cheap for them to do but it is still worth paying the extra money so that your guns, documents and pictures don't turn brown or become otherwise destroyed in a fire.

WHEN TO BUY
If you wait until the next big riot or fire to buy your gun safe, you're going to pay more because safes are hot commodities during times of unrest. I have usually found the best gun safe

prices between Thanksgiving and Christmas; however, if this is your first gun safe, I wouldn't bother waiting for that season since your valuables are currently not safe. It's not worth the risk. Besides that, if you're allowing for a higher budget for your safe, you're probably not going to have an extra thousand dollars at Christmastime, so that might not be the best time of year for you to buy if you're on a budget. Also, keep in mind that because you intend to hide your safe, scratch and dent sales or discounts are your new buddy.

THREE TYPES OF GUN SAFE LOCKS

There are three different types of gun safe locks. The first is the *traditional dial*. These are tried-and-true and will work even if there's an EMP or other event that destroys electronics. The downside is there a pain in the neck to get into, especially if you're in a hurry. I've lost count of how many times I have opened the safe taking something out, closed the safe only to realize seconds later that I needed to get back in and grab something else. This gets pretty annoying with a dial-type lock. Also, you'll notice that if you have a dial-type lock, you don't tend to use the safe much for things that you need to get to on a regular basis because it's not worth the hassle of constantly locking and unlocking the safe.

Electronic locks such as the pushbutton electronic type are much easier and more convenient to get into, so if you're planning on getting into your safe on a regular basis, you may want to consider these. They tend to have a code that is resettable so that you can make it something that has meaning to you. When setting the code, make sure that it is something obscure; don't make it your birthday, or your kid's birthday, or your address, or anything else that will be easily guessed. Something to keep in mind if you are purchasing a safe with an electronic lock is that the entry-level price range safes typically have a less reliable lock on them. Some of the small gun safe stores in our area can't compete with the prices of the big box stores, but if you buy the cheapest safe at the big box store, the local safe company is still making a pretty good living because they often have to come out and replace the electronic locks on these cheaper safes after a year or two. It's easy to find the lock to avoid, simply go to a store and look at the $200 or $300 safes. The lock on the front of that safe is the one you're trying to avoid. When using pushbutton safes, it's very important that after you open the safe, you push the rest of the buttons that are available, this way you don't wear down only the buttons that show your code, or leave residue on the buttons that open the safe.

EMP LOCKS

Some manufacturers are now putting what they call EMP locks on their safes. The safes have both a dial and an electronic push button combination. The idea here is that you'll have the convenience of a pushbutton lock, but if for some reason the electronic lock doesn't work, you'll have the back up of being able to open the safe using the traditional dial.

WHERE TO KEEP SAFE CODES

Not on the back of the safe or in a drawer with the title, " gun safe code" written next to it. Consider turning your gun safe code information into an obscure sentence. For instance, if my code was 19, 87, 39 maybe I'll write it down as, " In nineteen eighty-seven, J. Smith turned thirty-nine. This way I have the code and also a slight clue. The next thing I want to do is place this where I'll be able to find it, but somewhere that doesn't seem out of place from other papers. For example, if I were to take that sentence, write it on a piece of paper and tape it to the wall on the opposite side of the room from the safe, it would be pretty obvious what that was for. Next, I want to make a duplicate of that paper and give it to somebody that I trust, such as a close family member who lives at a different address. Have that person place the paper in a safe place such as their gun safe or safety deposit box or the glove box of their car. It should be fine there because it's far enough away from your house, and safe as long as the person doesn't write, *"This is Joe Smith's gun safe directions"* on it; people won't be able to make the connection.

Speaking of directions, if it's a dial safe, you need to turn it three times to the right, two times the left, once to the right, that sort of direction could also work into a sentence to make it sound like you've written down directions to get to a gun store. For instance, *"Hardware store directions"*: Make a right at the light on Second street, then a left on S. Way and a right on Wesson Street at the red light—something like that. You may choose to leave directions or the code to your safe with someone you trust in case they need to get into it someday for you, or in case you lose your code, or in case they are an executor of your will. You'll want to bring this person over to your safe at some point and have them open it several times since they are a little tricky at first. Choose wisely, make sure you pick someone that knows this: a secret is information disseminated to one person at a time. You don't want to give this code to someone who will then entrust it to someone else who shares it with a third person who you don't trust.

HOW BIG OF A SAFE DO YOU NEED?
In a word, bigger. I see many people make the mistake of thinking, *well I only have five guns so I'll get a 10 gun safe*. The reality is, by the time that 10 gun safe gets to your house, there's already a stack of papers, documents, pictures and other valuables that you'll want to put in that gun safe along with your guns, not to mention the fact that the price of ammunition is so high that you could easily have a collection of ammunition that exceeds the price of the gun itself. Nowadays most people want to lock up ammunition as well, because of all this you're going to need a lot larger safe than you assume. Also, if the safe is jam packed, you won't want to take anything out of it because it'll be a hassle to unload it to get to whatever is in the back.

52

You want a safe that's large enough that things can set in there and you can still reach things in the back without having to unpack the stuff in the front to get to it.

TOOLS

These days, it's very common to find an 18 Volt cordless grinder with cutoff wheels or a sawz-all that will cut right through the side of the safe. If you own one of these tools, don't leave it out. I would recommend keeping your cordless grinder, or anything else that will cut through the sides of your safe inside of the safe itself.

HUMIDITY

Humidity can kill guns in a hurry so it's important that you keep the humidity down inside of your gun safe. This can be accomplished with desiccant packs. The ones I prefer have a 110 plug in on the side of a plastic box full of colored desiccant beads. The purpose of the plug is that you can take the desiccant container out of the safe when the desiccant bead color indicates they are wet and plug it into the wall. A small heater in the desiccant pack will drive the moisture off of the beads. Then you simply unplug it and place the desiccant pack back inside the safe. You can also use heat rods and electric dehumidifiers.

ALARMS

After reading what I just wrote about tools being able to penetrate a safe, obviously we need to take steps to avoid leaving someone enough time to cut through your safe. This is where a house alarm comes in, and it doesn't have to be anything extravagant. We want to give burglars the understanding that they will not have time to stand around and cut through your safe. Remember that avoiding burglaries is somewhat like bear racing: you don't have to be faster than the bear, you just have to be faster than the other people the bear is chasing! The way this works with burglaries is that if your home looks like a more difficult target than your neighbor's home, you're less likely to get hit. Be careful about making it look like you have a lot of expensive goodies that someone might want to take the risk to acquire.

— Chapter 4 —

EXTRA EQUIPMENT: PROS AND CONS

PEPPER SPRAY

LET'S BEGIN WITH PEPPER SPRAY; Pepper spray is a nice tool but it is no replacement for a handgun. Pepper spray may be one alternative if you were forced to be in an area that does not allow handguns. As I said, it is no replacement, but it would be better than nothing. I have used pepper spray extensively over the years while on duty. It is an intermediate use of force on a level more serious than pushing and shoving, but below the use of force level of a handgun. Just so you have an understanding of how seriously the law views the use of pepper spray, officers have what is called a "use of force" chart. On that chart, as the use of force escalates above physical holds (pushing, using pain compliance holds, or wrestling someone down) the next level of force is at the officer's discretion: it is either pepper spray or his baton. You will not be caring a baton, but this gives you an indication of just how serious the situation needs to be before pepper spray is deployed. I've seen it temporarily halt people in their tracks and have also seen people who were almost completely immune to it. I found this especially to be the case with people who eat a lot of Hispanic food or other spicy foods that include red pepper. Pepper spray's main ingredient is the oil from a common red pepper. I have had Hispanic partners for instance who can spray a rolling fog of pepper spray into a trashcan, dunk their head in it, talk to me, and come up with little more than slightly red eyes. I'm just the opposite. When I used the stuff, I suffered for hours. Not that I couldn't work through it because once you train yourself you can force yourself to keep your eyes open and keep working, although with limited vision due to constant tears in your eyes and limited breath and snot running out of your nose. I'm sure we have all

54

had the unfortunate experience of getting poked in the eye. Do you remember how hard it was to keep your eye from clamping shut? It was very hard, but it was possible. If someone needed to look into your eyes to see if there was damage, you could force yourself to hold your eye open. Pepper spray is very similar, only it's not even as bad as getting poked in the eye. You can force yourself to hold your eyes open and you can continue to work through it.

Pepper spray does not work immediately. If you use pepper spray on someone, first spray and then run back and to one side. Do not retreat in a straight line. The reason is because even as this irritant takes effect, the assailant usually will start lunging forward and swinging his fists wherever he saw you last. Also, using pepper spray is serious. If you use it when you're not in eminent danger of great bodily injury, you could be charged with assault with a caustic chemical, which is a felony. So using pepper spray should be done almost as judiciously as using a firearm. Also, if you decide to use pepper spray, receive proper training for its use. The training should not only cover use of the pepper spray, gaining familiarity with it including getting a dose of it yourself, but should also include first aid instruction.

The reason first aid instruction is important is that some people who are exposed to pepper spray may then have difficulty breathing that becomes life threatening. This may become important if you accidentally spray someone, especially people who already have compromised breathing for any of several medical reasons. Decontamination for pepper spray includes copious amounts of moving air. Usually the best thing you can do is turn a common fan on high and stare at it. Water is alright, but not terribly effective because the pepper spray is an oil base, and the water runs right off of it, unless you are also using soap to release the oil. What you definitely do not want to do under any circumstances when decontaminating from pepper spray is use warm or hot water. Doing so is like throwing gasoline on a flame because the warm or hot water causes the pores of your skin to open, which drastically increases the discomfort from the pepper spray. Also, be aware of where the water is draining. If you're letting the contaminated water run off your face, down your shirt and onto the front of your pants, you will not be happy.

Pepper spray is also commonly used as a tool of torture. This would happen by restraining a victim and spraying it into their ear (not that we would ever do this), needless to say, don't get it in your ear or you will have a bad day! You also need to be careful not to jump into a car and start driving immediately after deploying pepper spray. I used it for training out at our local sheriff's department range one time and then got in my car to drive away. I had to slam on the brakes because the effects suddenly returned.

When you start carrying multiple levels of force, i.e. pepper spray and a gun, and if you decide to use the gun, expect to be second-guessed as to why you chose the gun over the pepper spray. It's mainly used by law enforcement to stop physical altercations. You don't know how well it's going to work, or how long it will take before it takes effect. Trusting your life to those odds is taking a big chance.

I do recommend carrying pepper spray for people who have concerns about dogs. All it takes is a little squirt on the nose and the dog will be busy nose surfing on the ground for a while. The dog would need to be an eminent threat, otherwise you may be charged with animal cruelty.

A handful of places commonly restrict pepper spray on the premises. Please make sure it's legal to carry. Hospitals are a great example. If someone used pepper spray in the hospital and it got inside the air ducts, it would very likely endanger those already hospitalized with breathing problems.

Another concern with pepper spray is that the pressure can leak off from the can. To avoid this, replace the can annually. You'll want to switch it out even more often if you have pressed the button and released any spray. The valves on the cans are more prone to leak pressure off slowly after they have been used. When using pepper spray don't spray it only at the assailant's eyes. Ideally when targeting, you start by spraying toward the chest and then quickly elevate to the top of the head. This tends to catch the people in the face who duck when they see it coming. Almost everyone ducks.

If you decide to use pepper spray, be aware of your local laws because they vary as to what percentage of OC (red pepper oil) you are allowed to have. For instance, in California, you can currently carry pepper spray with a content of up to 10% OC. When you're shopping, you'll find lots of Pepper spray with a 5% OC blend. It would stand to reason that 5% OC would find a larger group of people who were unaffected or not sufficiently affected by it.

STUN GUN

The term stun gun is slightly misleading because the stun gun is not a gun at all; it doesn't fire or project anything. It would be more accurately described as a stun stick or stun box. It's basically a battery with a coil that increases the voltage housed in a plastic box. The box has two small metal tabs on the front. When you touch somebody with the metal tabs and press the button, it shocks them with very high voltage yet with low amperage. This disrupts the use of muscles up to a few seconds on most people. On our use of force chart this would be similar to using pepper spray. It can be a good deterrent, but like pepper spray, a stun gun will not replace your gun. They do work great for dissuading dogs and the nice thing is you don't even have to touch them with it. Dogs can't stand the snapping sound of the electricity, so usually that's enough to send them away.

Some concerns with stun guns include the fact that you have to be within arms reach to use it. You also need to get it to bare skin or thin clothing which tends to be problematic in the winter or when the bad guy is swinging his fists at you. If the other person is more dexterous than you, it may just be knocked out of your hand before you can use it effectively because again you have to be within arms reach to use it. Also, you have to be careful with the batteries on these things. I've had some with rechargeable batteries that have not only gone dead, but failed to ever recharge after just a month or two, so do your homework before purchasing if you decide you want one. As with pepper spray, check your local laws to ensure it's legal in your area. Usually if it is legal in your area your local gun stores will sell them, but it's always good to double check with your local Sheriff's Office.

TASERS

Tasers work similarly to stun guns except that they actually fire two small darts attached to wires into the skin of the assailant before delivering the electric shock. Obviously the upside here is that you don't have to be within arms reach of the assailant for this to be effective; many Tasers will fire the darts 15 feet or more. The downside is that you typically only get one shot. Also, just like stun guns and pepper spray, the effectiveness varies depending on the assailant, especially if he's on drugs like meth. Some people will drop to the ground like a sack of potatoes and wet themselves. Others will just stand there staring at you and then attack. The effectiveness can also vary depending on clothing. If he's wearing a heavy leather jacket, the barbs are likely not going to make it to his skin. They also tend to be a little more bulky than stun guns. Most Tasers are roughly the size of a handgun. Since we know that a Taser is no replacement for a gun, this would mean that if you decide to carry both, it's going to be a bulky combination. You may choose to carry this where guns aren't allowed. Just like the stun gun, you need to be careful and ensure the battery is both reliable and charged. Check local laws to learn whether they are legal in your area. Never carry the Taser near your gun. You don't want to get those mixed up while responding.

KNIVES

I've lost count of how many people I've seen loaded into an ambulance on their way to the hospital with knife wounds, often with multiple wounds. Usually, it looks really bad because there's a lot of blood. I've seen guys loaded into an ambulance that I thought would never make it to the hospital, and then find out they were released the next day. This is not to say a knife is not a serious weapon, but the effects usually do not quickly incapacitate the attacker, and like the stun gun, it requires that you be within arms reach.

A knife is not a replacement for a gun. Almost every time I've seen a knife used in a fight after Mr. Knife Man gets one or two slashes in, it gets knocked out of his hand. From there on out it turns into a fistfight. This is why before a premeditated knife attack, many attackers who know what they are doing will put the knife in their hand and then wrap tape around the hand locking it in place. Apparently, it's pretty hard to find the knife on the ground when the other guy is punching you in the head. Keep in mind that if the assailant is much larger than you, there's a chance you just provided the knife that is going to be used on you. You also need to know the basics of knife fighting and practice if you are expecting to protect yourself with a knife. Often during breaks I cover the correct way to fight with a knife during our DefenseSHOT Advanced Shooting class. It's interesting to note that using a knife is often seen as less civil than using your gun.

FLASHLIGHTS

Flashlights are great to have with you, and they don't have to be large. Although, if they are large they also afford you the ability to use them as a blunt force object if your life is in danger. If you've ever noticed, most cops hold the flashlight in their non-gun hand just above their shoulder. The reason we're holding it there is so we can bonk an assailant with it if necessary to save our life. It's already in the cocked position. If you need to use your gun and flashlight at the same time, try to keep the flashlight at arms length up and off to one side so that if he shoots at the light you're less likely to get hit. This is why we don't usually hold it with our wrists crossed like you see in the movies. Doing that would put the light in line with your head and chest. If he shoots at your light he's got ya.

If you're using a flashlight while also holding a gun, you want to hold the light with just your two strong fingers close to the front of the flashlight and your pinky and ring finger extended ahead of the lens. The reason you want to do this is so that you can control how much light you are using by shrouding the lens. If you're gun and flashlight are in use, you're going to want to be sneaky. Holding the flashlight in this manner allows you to shroud the light and use only the amount of light that is necessary for each situation as you move, instead of just being able to turn it on and off. If you're using the light on full blast, you are lighting yourself up if the light is bouncing off of anything around you. You are also ruining your night vision. Imagine standing on the curb in front of a dark house and watching someone walk through the house from room to room with a flashlight on. You know exactly where the guy with the flashlight is because he's lighting up the room that he's in. You also know the direction and speed of his movement based on all of the movement of the shadows that are cast as the flashlight moves. Using your light sparingly makes you stealthier and also spares your night vision. You remember going camping and waiting for your eyes to adjust so that you could see all the tiny little stars in the sky until some dork walked up with his flashlight and ruined your night vision? It takes a while for it to come back, doesn't it? If you're in a low light situation, you want to use your light sparingly so that you are not ruining your night vision. Also consider winking. This means that you're closing your shooting eye when using your flashlight on bright, and opening it only in low light. Don't worry you'll open it automatically if you need to shoot. Closing your shooting eye when using the light on bright will help save your night vision in that eye.

WEAPONS LIGHTS

A weapons light is a small flashlight clamped onto your gun. The upside of the weapons light is that it allows you to have one hand free to open doors, grab things, etc. while using your light and gun. If you were using a separate flashlight you would have to turn it off and tuck it close to your armpit each time you need your non-shooting hand to be free. Having a hand free is a big upside. The downsides are that you tend to muzzle, or point the gun at everything that you want to light up which is dangerous. It's also impossible to shroud the light as described in the flashlight section. Another big downside with weapons lights is that if a bad guy sees the light and decides to shoot at the light, it is almost certainly in line with your chest and head. That's less than ideal. Also, it effectively makes the size of the gun much larger and makes it difficult to find a holster that fits.

BACKUP GUN

Backup gun is a term meaning you are carrying a second gun in addition to your primary gun. A common saying is "the fastest reload is a second gun". Maybe if we are talking revolvers, but even then it's debatable. Especially since the backup gun is concealed in a secondary location. If you think you need to carry a second gun incase your primary gun malfunctions, buy a more reliable primary gun.

LASERS

I have lasers on a few of my CCW guns, but I am not using them for aiming. I have them as a deterrent. The little red or green laser dot waving around out in front of you takes a second to find, even on paper. Now imagine that moving dot is on a moving three-dimensional surface – the assailant and/or whatever is in his background. You can find your standard gun sights much faster. Unless your vision is so bad that you can't see your sights at arms length, they don't make much sense for sighting. Besides that, once you go through our DefenseSHOT Defense Shooting Class, you won't even need sights. Yes, really. You'll be proficient at instant target acquisition. Which is a way of saying, you'll be able to pull the gun up from your hip and aim dead on, on a one inch target, at seven yards without using your sights. That alone is a priceless skill when you have no time and your life is on the line. Another part of our Defense Shooting class is training you to shoot where you think.

You'll get good enough at this that in most cases you'll be able to shoot rapid fire and keep all shots on target even with your eyes closed. (There are additional safety precautions taken while you're shooting rapid fire with your eyes closed in our defense shooting class.)

Most students are able to do this so proficiently by the end of the defense shooting class that they could literally shoot a qualifying score for their CCW test rapid fire with their eyes closed. You can imagine what this does for your speed and ability when shooting at moving targets and multiple targets or when shooting without your glasses or in low light. So there's no need to use a laser for aiming. Then why have a laser on your gun? It's because there have been many cases where suspects were being held at gunpoint and continue to act foolishly until they noticed a laser dot moving around on their chest. Sometimes it just helps drive the point home. This is why I don't mind spending a few hundred dollars on a nice laser. You never know when it might help make the point, and cause the assailant to stop the attack, so that you are not forced to shoot him.

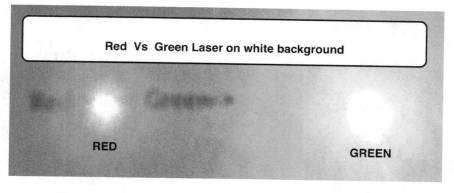

Red Vs Green Laser on white background

RED   GREEN

If you were going to buy a laser, I highly recommend getting green lasers, not red ones. Red lasers are almost invisible in bright sunlight. Green lasers seem many times brighter and are easier to find in bright light, although because of the State restrictions on how bright the laser can be, even the green laser can be difficult to find in bright sunlight. Normally, when someone brings a red laser out to our shooting facility for the first time and tries to use it during the day they can't understand why their laser won't come on; It's on, it's just useless during the day.

Another thing to remember about lasers is that they work both ways. In other words, that bright light that you're seeing out ahead of you will look even brighter coming from the assailant's point of view. So you wouldn't want to be using a laser if you're trying to stay hidden. If you are going to purchase a laser consider where it is mounted. There are companies out there that make nice lasers except that they are mounted directly above your right hand. The problem with this is when your finger is indexed above the trigger, as it should be until you're ready to shoot, your finger is blocking the laser. Also, consider what this laser means for your choice of holsters. Many times putting a laser on the gun drastically reduces the amount of choices you have for holsters. If the laser is mounted ahead of the trigger guard it is also going to make the profile of the gun more round. The problem with making the profile more round or square rather than the standard gun profile where the barrel or slide extend ahead of the trigger is that unless you have a really well-designed holster the new shape adversely affects retention of the gun. In other words, a round or square gun is going to roll out of the holster easier than a long, narrow gun.

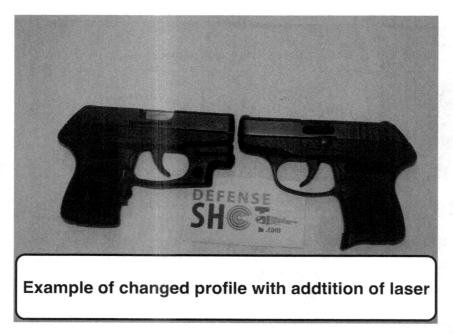

Example of changed profile with addtition of laser

There is at least one laser manufacture out there that makes a laser that is designed to replace the recoil spring guide rod in your semi-automatic. The upside of this laser is that you don't need a different holster. The downsides are that they are more expensive, not quite as bright, and of the two I have one that has failed twice. I contacted the company and they replaced it the first time, then the new one lasted a couple of months before it failed. I have the same laser in another gun and it still working fine after many years. Needless to say, I'm not thrilled with that company—Laser Max. Great design, not so great quality in my experience.

Green lasers are priced higher than red lasers. The green laser is a newer technology. A green laser will use the battery roughly five times as fast as a red laser. This isn't a big deal because the red laser might last a few hours and the green laser might last 20 minutes, it's still going to be more time than you'll need it. Another consideration when purchasing a laser is how the laser turns on. Some designs turn the laser on as soon as you grip the gun tightly. These designs usually have a small pressure switch-type button that is placed on the back strap or on the grip directly below the trigger guard. These are nice because they are an instinctive. Others such as the one on the lasers that are housed inside the buffer spring usually employ the use of a button on the side of your slide above the trigger.

Other laser designs that house the laser ahead of the trigger guard typically have a push button on the side of the laser housing ahead of the trigger. The lasers that have a button you are going to reach for with your trigger finger have one downside: even at the range, people sometimes accidentally press the trigger thinking they were pressing the laser button. You'll hear a bang. You'll see a hole in the target, and then see the startled look on the shooter's face because they intended to activate the laser, not press the trigger. It would be reasonable to assume that someone would be even more likely to make this mistake when they are under the stress of a life or death situation. Firing prematurely is not appreciated.

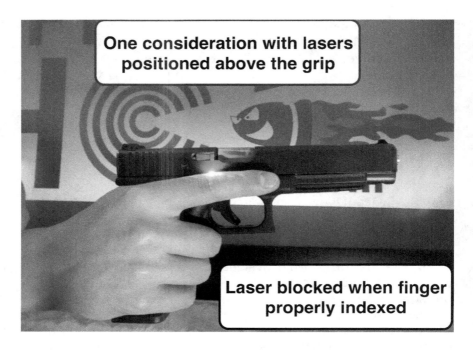

One consideration with lasers positioned above the grip

Laser blocked when finger properly indexed

Aiming a new laser added to your gun is simple. First make sure your gun is unloaded and pointed in a safe direction with your finger off the trigger. Then look down the sights. Activate your laser with one hand on the gun. Use your free hand to adjust the tiny Allen head screws that aim your laser. One for up /down and the other for right / left. Move the laser dot on the wall until the dot is at the tip of your front sight when your sights are aligned. Now move the laser dot down so that you can barely see the top edge of the laser dot at the top of your front sight. The laser is now aligned with your factory sights. 25 feet is the optimum distance to set the laser so that it matches your sights for defense purposes. Be gentle with the adjustment tool. These tiny Allen heads are delicate so if you start to feel extra resistance as you turn the adjustment, stop.

NIGHT SIGHTS

Night sights are great. Many guns on the market today allow you to purchase factory installed night sights for around $80. It's a good investment for a couple of reasons. First off, obviously you can use your sights in low light. Now we've already discussed that once you're trained in our Defense Shooting class you won't really even need sights in a defensive shooting situation. However, this will still allow you to have the option if you like. Maybe someday you'll need to take a long distant shot in the dark. Night sights turn your 12-hour gun into a 24-hour gun.

The other really nice benefit of night sights is that it's easy to find your gun in the dark as long as you're behind it. So if you're the kind of person that places your holstered CCW gun on the nightstand next to you while you're sleeping and it is pointed away from you—which it should be anyways—it's easy to find. If it's a gun without night sights on the nightstand in the dark, you'll be slapping the top of the nightstand to locate your gun. If it has night sights, you'll know right where it is, and go straight for the grip. This benefit alone is well worth the $80.

Night sights in the dark. Gun laying holstered on nightstand

— Chapter 5 —

HOW DO YOU LEARN? HOW DO YOU TRAIN?

DIFFERENT MOTIVATIONS WORK FOR DIFFERENT PEOPLE. For instance, when I tell my wife she can't hit a target she seems to hit it dead center. She once had a professor tell her she should stay away from Chemistry. That pushed her hard enough to excel and go onto Pharmacology College where she set many records over her 30-year career. You push someone hard enough, most of the time they'll surprise even themselves. However, a strait up challenge or drill Sargent style of push is not the correct approach to motivate and train most people. For most students reassurance that they can hit the target, and learning with zero stress is the best approach. External stress is only added well after they are confident and competent.

Think about this for a second: The difference between reality and fiction is that fiction must seem plausible, whereas reality does not need to seem plausible. What you think is possible or plausible is largely dependent on preconceived ideas whether right or wrong. Everything you've learned in life is solely dependent on information you've gathered. Some of that information could have been wrong.

For my wife, Heather, it's slightly different. Her motivator is not someone saying it's difficult—instead her motivator is someone saying it's difficult for her, which is a challenge. Other people may simply respond by accepting that it's difficult and just give up. Assuming a task is difficult to do only makes it harder. With me training you, shooting is not difficult. I regularly train brand-new beginners who have never touched a gun before, and within an hour they can shoot accurately. Within three hours, they've committed these new skills to their subconscious and are able to rapid-fire onto multiple targets with precision. With four hours of training I could put them in a friendly competition up against most of my former partners and they would hold their own. Most of my students would dominate. I've had students with six or seven hours of training go straight into competition level shooting and do well. I have other students with six hours of training go and talk with other cops about their training. The officers were amazed not only of their ability, but also at the scope of training they had received in such a short period of time. I've even heard some cops say they haven't been trained to the level DefenseSHOT offers.

Shooting is not difficult if you're trained correctly. If you're trained incorrectly, then of course it becomes difficult. There's an analogy I like to use: If I trained a driver on a racetrack, (which I used to do) and glued his hands at the bottom of the steering wheel, that would make his job difficult. With that being said, if I gave him reassurance and told him to put his hands at 3 and 9 o'clock, there job instantly becomes easier

Part of the secrets of our students being able to make such huge leaps in such a short amount of time is proper training. If you learn this incorrectly, it will be much more difficult to train your brain to change its ways. It's important we catch any problems as soon as possible so they can be corrected. A person who has learned poorly will have a harder time to correct their habits than an individual who has never shot before and has no experience. This is one reason I often tell people its better not to go out and do a bunch of shooting on your own before coming to class. When you take our training and learn right the first time, you'll spend far less money on the ammunition learning faster, and won't pick up any bad habits in the process. When you look at it this way, the training we offer saves you money! You're burning money on ammunition or learning how to shoot incorrectly. It's more affordable to learn it right the first time.

People not properly trained will normally go out shooting one afternoon and easily burn through $100, $200 or more worth of ammunition and never realize they haven't improved. When training with us at DefenseSHOT, you have supervision to ensure you're not picking up any bad habits along the way. You'll shoot less ammo, and make far greater gains in your shooting skills than you ever could on your own.

Even people who are—successful make sure they get coaching on a regular basis. When the top businesses in the world bring in people for seminars to teach them how to run a business, they get even better. The only person who can't learn is the person who thinks they already know everything. We have all met those type of people that seem to know everything and can't take in any new information.

The difference between better and best is to continue training and continue to be coached. You want to be very confident with your skills. If you get into a *fair fight* your tactics are terrible. You want to be good enough in your skills where there isn't a fair fight and you will be the clear victor because we are talking about a contest of life or death. There is no second place winner and there is no such thing as a fair fight if you are stopping someone trying to murder you or others. Our intent is never to kill anyone. We want to be able to confidently and competently stop the imminent threat of anyone trying to kill others. So for us, *winning the fight* simply means stopping the threat. Often, the best way to win the fight is to not be in the fight in the first place. In another chapter, we'll discuss how to read your surroundings. Often this will keep you out of trouble in the first place, and if it doesn't, at least it will allow you to see the trouble before it gets to you so you have time to react.

We have other cutting edge training that is just now being introduced and used in large law enforcement agencies. (They are usually the only ones who can afford these computer programs and hardware.) These agencies (and you) can train with us in the evenings standing in front of a life-size movie screen that's playing out a real life scenario. You will decide in each scenario *when* and/or *if* you need to react, and how to react in real time. The program will respond to your inputs so if you shoot or don't shoot, it will change the scenario. If you shoot and miss, or shoot and hit, it will change the scenario as it continues. Once you've completed the scenario, we will debrief with two veteran retired peace officers to see what you did and if we could've done things any differently. This training is invaluable and it's also a lot of fun! There is no age limit on this class so feel free to invite anyone who'd like to have fun and learn. This is the best way to safely learn how to handle split second decisions and get experience doing so without actually being in harm's way. You'll also be able to watch others as they go through scenarios, which is both educational and entertaining. Many students will specifically focus on training and enjoy the class at that level and others who are competitive will probably want to keep a score with their friends or family when they come as a group. Either way, it will be a lot of fun. There are hundreds of scenarios available from standing in a convenience store, to being attacked while you are in your car. We build scenarios and continue to add them. The variety is endless so you can continue to come back. Also, we continue building timely video scenarios from current events. When we learn of another shooting or another incident that's been in the news, we can re-create the scenario to see how we react. You'll be able to place yourself in the moment.

Our program will show you how to draw your gun, proper trigger compression, alignment and even accuracy within every scenario. In addition, the program measures your reaction time within fractions of a second. Think of it as a sophisticated flight simulator for Cops. This will allow you to learn how to react in life-and-death decisions in a split second but also work on your target shooting holster draw and other critical skills simultaneously.

When you train with us at DefenseSHOT, the person sitting next to you is often the head of a government department or even a Superior Court Judge. There's a world of difference between training with us versus training with a gun store or someone who just happens to like guns. There's no replacement for law-enforcement experience. As important as that is, it's only part of the equation for us. It's important to know that if you have a God-given gift in the form of a talent or ability, the gift is not for you, it's for others. In my case, my talent, my gift has always been teaching. It's my responsibility to share that gift and improve on it so that you receive the best possible training and can learn as quickly and entertainingly as possible.

Over the past three years I've won seven, "Best Firearms Instructor awards." Every time I conduct a class, I debrief afterwards and see how I could make it better so the classes evolve and improve over time. This is why it's not uncommon for me to talk to a Superior Court Judge, or the head of a government department during a break or after class and ask them what they thought. I often get the response that it was perfect. I'm not bringing this up to bolster myself, but rather to bolster you. When you come through our classes you can walk away confident that you received the very best training possible. Some may think that a difficult test at the end of the course indicates that you have had the best training. I disagree. I think that the best training means that you have the best training. I've had over 1000 hours of law-enforcement training before the age of 20. This was followed by thousands and thousands of hours training during my career. Including different forms of martial arts and even being a driving instructor. I've trained everyone from kids on the freeway to people at the racetrack. Even Peace Officers at the CHP Academy EVOC (Emergency Vehicle Operations Course) facilities. I suspect I'm qualified to make an assessment regarding which training methods work best. In our classes—the ones that don't have mandatory tests—you'll have plenty of opportunities to test yourself and push yourself to your limits to see how good you have become and how much you know. I feel this is a superior training model. Instead of having students simply meet test expectations, we end up with students that far exceed any test expectations or requirements. This is why our students easily breeze through even the classes that have mandatory tests. There is a reason why of the thousands of CCW students we have trained to date, we have never had a student be denied a CCW. This philosophy is derived from two biblical concepts: the difference between the old way and the new way.

Many of the techniques and philosophies that we use in our DefenseSHOT training are derived from biblical concepts though we don't discuss it in class the way I have touched on it in this book. In class, students are a captive audience. I'm sensitive to that. Whereas in a book, it's easy to skip a line or two if you like. (Although you might lose some context). Keep in mind that the topics covered in this book are here because so many students have asked me questions about these topics after class. So when I touch on topics including scripture references in this book, please keep in mind that they are here by popular demand.

— Chapter 6 —

APOLOGETICS FOR CCW

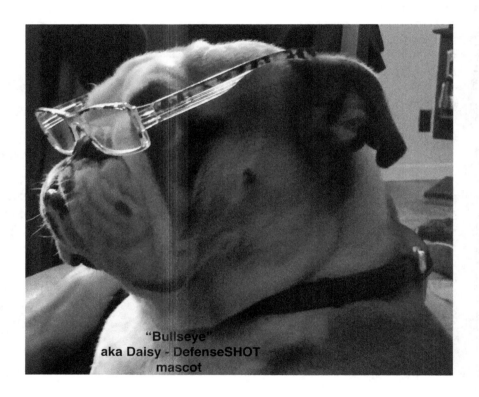

"Bullseye"
aka Daisy - DefenseSHOT
mascot

APOLOGETICS IS A TERM THAT HAS NOTHING TO DO WITH APOLOGIZING, but rather explaining and reasoning. When it comes to apologetics for CCW, I'll give you some ammunition to explain why a CCW is a great idea. I will also arm you to defend the Second Amendment. I have found that asking rhetorical questions, where the listener is led to the obvious conclusion, tend to be very effective. In order for it to be effective, your motivation must be that of someone who is trying to enlighten the listener. If your responses come across as some sort of contest, they will not be as effective when trying to persuade the listener.

Following are some examples of rhetorical questions to concerns regarding CCW. If someone were to ask you, "Why do you want to carry a gun? Are you looking for trouble?" I like to answer that question with the question, "Why do you wear a seatbelt? Are you looking for an accident?" You carry a gun not because you're looking for trouble, but instead, to be prepared when there is trouble. And not just any trouble, it would have to be an eminent threat of great bodily injury or death on an innocent victim. The bottom line is you don't have to be looking for trouble; trouble is looking for you. Much like a parachute, we hope to never need it. But if we need it and don't have it, we will never need it again.

If someone says you do not need to carry a gun because cops are available, ask them if they have a fire extinguisher at their house. If there are firemen, why do they need a fire extinguisher? It's because the firemen won't get there in time, but with a fire extinguisher they can either stop the fire or reduce the damage done. The same is true for cops and physical attacks. The statistics show that in mass shootings stopped by a CCW person, the number of persons shot is just over two. Now compare that with mass shootings where we are waiting for the cops to show up. The average number of people shot jumps up as high as 14. The average shooting is not a mass shooting. It involves two people and goes down in a couple seconds with two shots or fewer and under 21 feet in low light. What are the chances that a cop is going to be there within two seconds and within 21 feet? If he's any later than two seconds, or any farther away than 21 feet, then statistically, he's useless in the vast majority of attacks. A gun isn't heavy and not that difficult to carry; carrying a cop with you 24 hours a day, seven days a week is slightly more cumbersome.

Another common accusation you'll hear parroted is, "if everyone is carrying a gun, it will be like the wild, wild west and everyone will be shooting each other at the drop of a hat!" First of all, for those who watched too many movies it might come as a shock to know that most towns in the west did not allow you to carry a gun in town. Also, the statistics do not bear out their irrational fear that everyone will start shooting each other if they all have guns. Statistically, shoot outs between two CCW people are nonexistent, even though some cities, counties

73

and states have what anti-constitution people would consider alarmingly high numbers of concealed carriers. Sheriff John D'Agostini in California, along with a multitude of sheriffs from across the United States agree; "an armed society is a safe society". As the numbers of CCW carriers increases, the number of crimes drastically decrease. This is a statistic that is played out over and over across the United States.

Years ago, Florida decided to make CCW easily attainable and as a result the number of CCW carriers skyrocketed in Florida. What's fascinating about that is that shortly after that happened rental car agencies in Florida had to remove the rental car stickers and the license plate frames from the backs of their cars. They had to do that because they found that people who were driving rental cars were targeted. The rental car companies even gave instructions to people renting vehicles in Florida that if they were bumped from behind they were to continue driving and not to pull over. This is because the thugs assumed that if you were driving a rental car you were from out of state and would not be carrying a gun since you were not a Florida resident. They started bumping rental cars, causing the person to pull over to exchange insurance information and driver's license numbers, only to be attacked by the thugs who were comforted in their knowledge that the rental car driver did not have a gun.

Conversely, the areas with the highest gun crime rates are those that harshly restrict, or even deny, concealed carry to their residents. Chicago is a glaring example. Short of Mexico City, Chicago has one of the highest gun homicide rates in the Western world. For decades, Washington DC with no CCW was the homicide capital of the country. It shouldn't take a rocket scientist to figure out that when you tell people it's illegal to carry a concealed gun, the only people that will stop carrying, are law-abiding citizens. After all, if the bad guys followed the law, we could just make a law that you're not allowed to murder anybody. How about if we stiffen the penalty? How about we add another law and this time we call it the "We Really, Really Mean it now and We're Not Kidding; Don't Murder Anybody law". That should do the trick, right? There are already far more than enough laws on the books to keep people from attacking each other. Since criminals ignore laws, the people most affected by laws are law-abiding citizens, not criminals. Laws affect the people that are not causing trouble in the first place. When laws are enacted regarding your ability to protect yourself, it's a double whammy. Because not only are you left more vulnerable, but it becomes common knowledge to criminals that you are vulnerable, giving them the green light.

Posted gun free zones must be one of the most ignorant arrangements today. Putting up a gun-free zone sign is just as effective as sheep posting a, "No-Wolf Allowed Here" sign. This is why it's no coincidence almost all mass shootings happen in gun-free zones. The mass shooter who plans his hit will always consider how many targets he has available and how much time he has before he's stopped. "Gun free zones" have done all the thinking for him when it comes to the second criteria. If gun free zone signs work so well, why don't we just hang a gun free zone sign on the fence in front of the White House? Because of common sense, that's why. So why do "important" people get to be protected by guns, but our kids in schools get "protected" by a sign that announces the shooter will have 15 minutes or more before he is confronted? I submit that the reason is because there is a large portion of the population that does not understand the difference between thinking and feeling. To many, if it *feels* good it must be good. Ah, wrong. Feelings lie a lot. Ask any pilot or racecar driver. You have to trust your gauges even if they conflict with your feelings. That's also good dating advice for your kids.

Next is the argument that the Founders never knew about high-capacity magazines or rapid fire. They know because they have seen TV shows and movies that show guys with guns shooting one shot and then putting a stick down the barrel before shooting the next shot. The fact is there were guns with 20 round magazines developed 12 years before the Second Amendment was ratified. And you can also look up an early spending bill pushed by many of the same people who had just written the Second Amendment to order guns capable of shooting 20 rounds in less than two seconds. So the rapid fire that non-gun people most closely associated with a "machine gun" was already on the scene. The idea that the people who wrote the Second Amendment had no idea that guns would ever be capable of shooting more than one round at a time is preposterous.

The next argument is, "Well, yes but they of course meant you should only have small guns for hunting". First off, the Second Amendment has absolutely nothing to do with hunting, or sport, or tradition, as we will cover below. Secondly, as far as the size of guns, there was a famous letter written from a ship captain who made regular trips into the Caribbean. The captain mailed a letter stating that he had read the Second Amendment and wanted to know if it was okay that he had cannons on his ship because he was dealing with pirates in the Caribbean. The answer came back and it basically said, "Of course, that's what the Second Amendment is for!"

Now let's take a look at the Second Amendment. "Who am I to explain the constitution to you?" you ask. Do I have a Doctorate in Constitutional Law? No. I'm sure I can find two professors who would argue opposing points of view on the Second Amendment so clearly a Doctorate does not confirm an absolute understanding of its intention. What a doctorate does indicate is that someone has been indoctrinated. I took an oath to uphold the Constitution, which includes every person's individual rights. Those weren't just words for me. I studied to make sure that I upheld my oath. Protecting people's individual rights was even more important than catching bad guys. Also, I was entrusted to travel to the Soviet Union with the US State Department. For years, prior to doing that, and for a lifetime after, I have studied: history, governments, and social engineering. I'm also a student of scripture like the Founders were. This provides me a different perspective on humanity, history, social engineering, and government, in many ways, the same perspective that our Founding Fathers had. They weren't all Christians, but they definitely all studied the scriptures.

The Constitution is the flower of the Renaissance and the Bible is its seed. How ironic that so many today think of the Constitution as antiquated. In the perspective of human history, the Constitution is cutting edge and state-of-the-art. It is the newest idea. The forms of government others seek to water it down with are ancient and obsolete; most are nothing more than forms of neo-Feudalism.

So let's take a look at this beautiful petal in the flower of the Renaissance: Amendment II: "A well regulated militia, being necessary to the security of a free state, the right of the people to keep and bear arms, shall not be infringed." It's so short! Only one sentence. How on earth are people messing this up? Well, for starters, they changed the meaning of words. Did you know Webster's intent in writing his dictionary in the first place was to make certain that words did not change meanings? This was so people would not change the understanding of the Constitution. Let's start out with the word "regulated". Many today would have you believe that regulated means heavily controlled by a government agency or agencies. At the time the Second Amendment was penned, "Well regulated" meant well trained. If they said someone was a "well regulated swordsman" they didn't mean that he had all his paperwork and certification approved by multiple agencies with background checks, etc. They meant that the guy knew how to use a sword well. They enumerated your right in the Second Amendment to have the ability to train with weapons. That's something slaves or servants were not allowed to do. They wanted it very clear that *you* were a citizen, which is the highest title of the land. Not a servant or slave. You had the right to have weapons and the right to train well with them for your individual defense.

Remember that any right you don't enjoy is a right you don't really have. Once you've taken, "Defense Shooting and Advance Defense shooting," classes with Defense SHOT, you can consider yourself well regulated with handguns.

The next word is "Militia". This is a word that has been cleverly demonized and rebranded. Militia in context meant a group of individual citizens who banded together for defense. That is all. It was quite necessary and common at the time for militias to form to protect their village from attack. During the L.A. riots, many of the business owners in the Asian community protected their communities and their lives with firearms. As a result, many of their communities did not burn and many of their lives were saved. They acted together in groups for a common defense. A modern example of a militia. These were not people trying to break away into their own little country, as many today have come to think of militias from watching too much T.V. They were just people who gathered to defend themselves from a common threat, and they separated from being an armed group back into armed individuals as soon as the threat was gone.

Now, let's look at the next part, "being necessary for the security of a free state". There are those that would mislead you to believe that this means the government needed to enumerate their own right to have a federal military or that each of the states did. I have even seen this in current high school textbooks. First off, it says "state" not "States." That alone should be the end of the argument. Unfortunately, it isn't. This was not written for individual states or the National Guard. The fact that it's number two in the Bill of Rights and these rights are for citizens, (and not the government), would tell you that that argument insinuating that the intent was to give authority to the Federal government or even the individual states to have arms is nonsense.

Other places in the Constitution lay out the responsibilities for the government and its relation with each of the states. The Bill of Rights is the wrong place in the Constitution for that. This is number two out of ten amendments making up the Bill of Rights. How do we know it was the area reserved for individual rights and not governmental rights? Does the government need a right to: *free speech? The right to a trial by its peers? The right not to be searched without reasonable cause, and so on?* Just like when reading the Bible, always consider the context, not just the text. If you take the text out of context, you are left with a con. And being conned is exactly what's going on here by the anti-gun /anti-Constitution movement.

Lastly, the word "free" before state didn't just fall in there by accident. All states—all governments—had arms. The point here was that the founding persons—(just kidding)—fathers, had just won their freedom from the most powerful government and military on the planet using firearms that each person owned individually. In fact, it was the attempt to take away their individual guns that kicked off the Revolutionary War. They had put up with everything else and given up many rights and money before that. This would include having soldiers move into their homes and being, "shook down", robbed and even beaten by bands of British soldiers acting with impunity. Taking away their guns is where they drew the line. They realized that people without arms were servants or slaves, (they still are) and that in order to be free and maintain their individual freedom, they must all be individually armed. So the word free in that sentence is a huge giveaway as to the intent of the sentence. Also, keep in mind that they understood there is no such thing as collective rights, only individual rights. The smallest minority is the individual, so by protecting the individual, you have protected everyone including all minorities. As soon as you start protecting a group over an individual you have destroyed individual rights.

Okay, so we have addressed the first part, which is where most of the attacks on your Constitutional right are focused. Now let's take a look at the next part, "...the right of the people to keep and bear arms shall not be infringed." Here we go again: The Founding Fathers doubled down, focusing on who this was meant to address "the right of the people" not the right of each state, or the Federal Government. The right of each individual person "to keep". Does that mean have them taken away? Clearly not. To keep "and bear", which means to carry with you, not leave in a safe or locked up somewhere. "Shall not" which means, must never, "be infringed" Infringed means, any act that undermined, encroached on, or limited, a right and that's lost on those who tell you what size, color, and type of gun you can have, where you can place it, how many you can have, what kind of ammunition you can have... The list is endless!

Now let's read it again since we've used apologetics and cleared up the fog of fake news surrounding the Second Amendment. When you read it this time, it should be as obvious and plain as if someone hit you in the forehead with a brick: "A well regulated militia, being necessary to the security of a free state, the right of the people to keep and bear arms, shall not be infringed." It's perfectly clear when not muddied up by the static of preconceived notions, fake news, or confirmation bias, wishing it meant something else.

Now, as I've mentioned, I'm also a student of scripture. I mention this because I will quickly tackle the argument, *live by the sword; die by the sword* and tie it back into the Founding Fathers. Many insinuate by this that if you carry a gun you will get shot. (I won't turn this into a Bible study. I'll keep it short). Even if you're not interested in scripture, I encourage you to read this part because it is an example of what formed the opinions of our Founding Fathers. So at least read it for historical perspective. First off, this is found in the Book of Revelation, and the context is history written in advance regarding a period of time known as the Tribulation. It's not referring to everyday life like a proverb. Even if it were, the preceding line destroys the argument that many try to make by taking the scripture out of context. Taking tiny pieces of scripture out of context is what I call *bumper sticker theology*.

Let's take a look at a little more context. Because bumper sticker theology is often wrong. In Revelation 13:10 we read, "He that leadeth into captivity shall go into captivity: he that killeth with the sword must be killed with the sword. Here is the patience and the faith of the saints". Now, I won't write the rest of it here, but you can see this is in the middle of the Book of Revelation regarding the seven years where the Anti-Christ makes a seven-year peace covenant with Israel and then exactly three and a half years to the day into the deal, he breaks the covenant. Then he starts killing anyone who won't take his mark known as the mark of the beast. So the context here is that those who resist him are either killed fighting him or lead into captivity (and later have their heads chopped off.) You can see it's a very specific text regarding a very specific time. And in this case, there are only two options: die fighting, or die in bondage.

Now let's loop this around to the Founding Fathers. As mentioned, they were students of Scripture. As such, they would have been familiar with this concept. The take away here for them was: your choices ultimately are to fight or to be enslaved. Clearly, they chose to fight, which is why we are still enjoying the little vestigial freedom lingering from their endeavor, the payment made for themselves and their posterity so that they would not be in bondage. Again, remember their point of view when reading the Second Amendment. There are those who say, "*Well, that stuff doesn't happen anymore, so we don't need the Second Amendment.*" Really? Has the heart of man changed since Adam? No. People are no different today. Control freaks want to take dominion over other people. This never stops. It is as inevitable and relentless as water moving downhill. There are more slaves on the planet today than ever before in history. In America, the land of the free, we now have over 30,000 laws or regulations on the books, each of them, an attempt to control others in some way. Often we're hoodwinked into legislating away our own freedom one piece at a time. The study of human history in the Bible will show you the default position of man is bondage, and freedom is fleeting. That's why our Founding Fathers told us that the cost of freedom is eternal vigilance. They knew from their study of history that keeping free is a constant uphill struggle. Every moment you let your guard down, someone will begin to infringe upon liberty. Losing your freedom, inch by inch, it's a cinch. That's why it's so important to understand the tools of those who would take your rights and be constantly on guard against them. The Founding Fathers knew from their study of the Bible that the history of man goes in cycles: freedom breeds prosperity, prosperity breeds decadence and apathy. Apathy allows people to fall into enslavement, which is by far the longest phase of the cycle. Enslavement eventually breeds the will to fight for freedom and around we go. Where do you think we are on that cycle today?

— Chapter 7 —

HOW TO USE THE RESTROOM

MOST CCW PEOPLE CHOOSE TO CARRY a gun in a holster on their waistband or belt. This is the fastest draw, but it does create a tricky situation in the restroom. If you are going to be seated in a stall, make sure that your gun and holster are flopped into the seat of your pants as you assume the seated position. When your pants are unbuttoned, and belt undone, the heavy gun wants to flop to one side or the other. If the gun flops to the outside of the pants, it may be pointed back at you, it may touch the bathroom floor which is just gross, or if your holster doesn't have good retention, the gun could slide out on the floor or in the worst case scenario, could fall into the toilet water. Now, I know your first inclination would be to flush it and buy a new gun rather than pick it up, but we can't do that. The simple fix is to fold the gun holster in toward the seat of your pants, and the problem is solved. For those using the urinal, when you unbuckle your belt hold tension forward on both sides of the belt while standing so that the belt doesn't become loose and allow your gun to flop out away from your waist.

The next tips don't have to do with your gun falling out; it has to do with not getting sick. Remember to use napkins to turn off the faucet and to open the door on the way out. If you're carrying in a purse, or a man purse, "murse", do not set it on the bathroom floor or bathroom counters. Studies have found the same bacteria and nastiness on many people's kitchen counters that are present on public restroom floors. This is happening because people set the purse on the floor or counter in the public restroom then come home and set the purse on their kitchen counter, transferring the contamination. You wouldn't prepare dinner on a public restroom floor, so don't bring the public restroom floor to your kitchen.

— Chapter 8 —

WHEN TO CARRY
AND WHAT TO DO ABOUT FRIENDS AND FAMILY

Eric Daniels. Staff & CCW Holder

HOW DO YOU DECIDE WHEN TO CARRY YOUR GUN? If we knew when we needed a gun, we wouldn't need a gun. If you knew you were going to get attacked you would decline to show up for that appointment. Because you don't know when you'll need it, it's best to carry it as often as possible. Add to that, the way the world works. The way the world works the phone doesn't ring until you pour milk onto your cereal, or sit down with a nice hot meal. You only get a flat tire while running late on the way to an important event. The guy who just robbed the bank gets caught when pulled over for a broken taillight. So the way the world works, you're more likely to need your gun the day you leave it at home. I have seen two kinds of people coming through our CCW classes: those who intend to carry whenever possible, and those who only plan on carrying for certain occasions, like traveling through cities, or hiking. The people who intend to only carry on certain occasions usually do so only a few times until comfortable carrying. Once you get used to carrying you start to feel uncomfortable without it.

Years ago, many people didn't wear seatbelts and it seemed a bother to wear it. When you started to wear it, you were very aware of the seatbelt. Now you hardly notice it. If you were to drive down the freeway and suddenly take off your seatbelt you would feel naked. Packing heat is the same. At first you will be aware and focused on the gun, but it won't take long before you are comfortable with it, and like the seatbelt, you'll start to feel naked without it. You will be more aware of when you don't have your gun than when you do have it. For most people, the only times you won't be carrying, is when you're at a place that doesn't allow you to carry.

YOU ARE THE FIRST RESPONDER

What about carrying your gun around friends who are uncomfortable with guns? Easy: you don't need that kind of negativity in your life, get new friends. Just kidding. This is concealed carry, no one needs to know about it, but I've heard accounts over the years from students that their friend was uncomfortable having a gun around until a certain event happened. Stories like, "my girlfriends didn't like the fact that I had a gun until we were walking through a parking lot and these two creepy guys started to walk near us. After that, they were glad I had a gun. Now they want your beginner class and the concealed weapons license class." We could go into what Freud said about people who are afraid of weapons, but we don't need to go there. Suffice it to say, people who have an irrational fear of guns have been preconditioned. Usually a reality check, like the one above will do the trick to break preconditioning.

Alternatively, you can use "what if" scenarios with your friend. Something like this: *If you were at Place X and someone tried to kill you, or rape you, or kidnap you (or your kids) what would you do?* They might answer, "Well, I would stop them. *How?* Explain that in this scenario, they are outnumbered or outmuscled. If they say they would call the cops, point out that a response time under ten minutes would be a miracle. Then ask, *how long do you think it would take for this person who is attacking you to hurt you?* Continue to ask "what if" questions until they realize the futility of their responses. People are under the misconception that cops are the first responders. We even refer to them as first responders but it's not true. The first responder is the person being attacked. Whether that response is to competently handle the situation because you have been trained and are prepared, or to incompetently handle the situation because you were not adequately trained and prepared, or to give up and allow yourself or another to be killed.

People like this often project onto you. Because they are incompetent regarding guns, they assume that others are incompetent as well. Since they don't trust themselves to use it correctly, they don't trust others either. This mindset is a packaged deal, along with appealing to authority. This means that while they don't feel comfortable with the average person having a gun, they are perfectly comfortable with an officer having a gun. Since they appeal to authority, they trust authority figures. Explain that you received your official training from retired veteran Peace Officers at DefenseSHOT and passed our officially certified multi-award winning classes. Often that will bridge the gap and they will feel more comfortable. Don't show them your gun, since the sight of the gun may shut down their ability to think reasonably. The correct time for them to see a "real" gun for the first time is at the shooting facility, or in our classes. People prefer to be introduced to guns in a more structured environment.

You'll find that most, if not all of your friends and family (the ones you let know) are glad you carry. Encourage others you trust to get their CCW because we can't be with everyone at all times. Because an armed society is a safer society, the more armed, the more safe. As CCW numbers climb crime rates plummet. Most thugs think twice about attacking people if they think there's a good chance their prey, or someone close by, is armed. DefenseSHOT is set up to help everyone from Green Berets to people who have never touched a gun before. With our fun, stress-free, three hour beginner class, people can go from never having touched a gun before on Friday, to confidently fitting right into our CCW class on Saturday, usually more competently than those who have been shooting for years.

You need a code word for your gun. This is because you don't want your friend, or your spouse, or your kid, to suddenly blurt out "Hey do you have your gun with you today?" or, "Your gun is showing!" It's better if they have a code word; like "friend". If they want to ask you if you have your gun, they can ask, "is your friend with you?" Or, if your gun is peeking out under your garment they can say, "check your friend." Using the code word for gun will draw less attention from people within earshot. If you have small children, keep your CCW secret from them as long as possible. Little guys are very perceptive, so it won't be too long before they figure it out; but the older they are the better, because they're less likely to blurt out the fact and forget your code word. Also, if you have small children watch that gun like a hawk. If you have little kids running around you, a purse might not be the best choice. Under those circumstances, it's important to keep it as close as possible so that it will be immediately apparent to you if anyone gets near it. Many ladies find that bra holsters or other deep concealment holsters provide more security for this kind of situation.

— Chapter 9 —

ATTEMPTED CAR JACKING

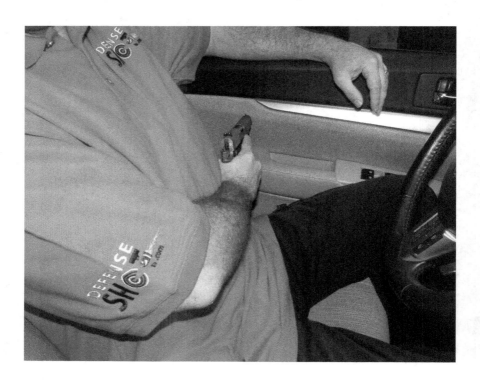

IN THE EARLY 90's, I WAS A ROOKIE COP. My wife and I decided to take a trip to Monterey for the weekend in our brand-new shiny red, four-wheel-drive Nissan standard cab truck. Looking at a map we decided to take the fattest lines on the map, which tend to be the primary roads. This took us through a certain Highway through a, "bad part of town," called Highway 4. In the early 90s, Highway 4 was a four-lane wide surface street with traffic lights through the middle of a dicey neighborhood: rundown buildings, heavy traffic and unpredictable people walking down the streets or loitering. It looked like a shady place to be even at 11 o'clock in the morning. As we got into the left turn lane pocket at a stoplight, to turn onto the on-ramp, we got stuck behind a vehicle at a red light and then another car pulled up behind us, so we were pinned in between the two. (Also, there was a Jersey barrier to our left and cars to the right). To my far left, I noticed a guy walking with the direction of traffic on his side of the road. He was carrying a small duffel bag with one hand on top and one hand hidden underneath the bag. He was looking directly at me as he walked. (I call it the target stare—looking with the same intent and indifference as a marksmen looking at a paper target). He didn't notice I was looking at him because I had sunglasses on and kept my head pointing straight ahead, even though I was looking to my far left, tracking him.

I watched him walking down the street, getting farther and farther into my peripheral and then behind me. From my vantage point, the only reason he was still in my peripheral view was I was breaking my eyeballs to look as far left as I could. I noticed he crossed two lanes of moving traffic. At that point, I could see him in my left-side view mirror as he leapt over the Jersey barrier and was advancing between the concrete wall and the stopped vehicles behind us. He was closing in on us and I decided to draw my full size duty sidearm (a stainless steel S&W .40 caliber 4006) and have it at the ready.

I un-holstered the .40 caliber, laid my left arm up on the windowsill, and with my right hand grasping the gun down in front of my belly, pointing out the door. One of many skills learned as deputies during the Sheriff's Academy in the event a culprit ever approached the driver's door of a patrol car. The suspect can't see the gun and (assuming you don't hit the one bar running through the door there for side impacts) the bullets travel right through the door should the suspect decide to pull a gun. I assumed he had a weapon in his hand since he was going out of his way to keep the hand concealed under the duffle, and he was coming up to carjack us, so I un-holstered because it was reasonable to assume he would be threatening our lives within seconds.

As he approached our truck and was almost to the back edge of my door he suddenly turned around and bolted. He ducked behind the truck, ran through two lanes of moving traffic that were slamming on their brakes and skidding to avoid him, and then disappeared between a couple buildings. I turned back around and noticed the vehicle in front of me was just starting to move. The light had turned green so I turned the corner and accelerated onto the onramp. Seconds later, my wife and I were equally amped up, our heart rates were through the roof, and she asked me, "What happened?!"

"*What happened?!*" I asked her, "Did you see that guy coming up alongside the truck?" She hadn't seen a thing outside our truck, and had no idea of the movements I'd been tracking. Baffled, I asked aloud, "I wonder what made the guy run away? He couldn't have seen the gun!" Heather confessed, "I never saw anyone. I heard your holster unsnap and saw you pull out your gun. I figured it was going to get loud, so I put my fingers in my ears…"

Heather's ear plugging hadn't escaped the assailant's attention. The hooligan didn't get to hurt us or threaten our life, but I'm pretty sure he got a new set of shorts out of the deal.

In hindsight, I realize I could have handled that situation even better. I was in rookie cop mode, trying to be sneaky. If instead of watching him out of the corner of my eye, I had looked squarely in his direction, to let him know that I was on to him, he may have avoided us in the first place.

— Chapter 10 —

HOW TO THINK LIKE A COP
HOW TO CARRY YOURSELF AND REACT

CARRYING YOUR LOADED GUN AND BEING PROFICIENT WITH IT are essential, the next most important thing you can do for your safety is to read your surroundings the way cops read our surroundings. Criminals count on us being sheep, being docile, this is often used to their advantage. We have to get out of this mindset of being polite to a fault. My father-in-law Donald Sutherland, a retired Green Beret, demonstrated one example of this to me. One time, I came up behind him and he didn't realize I had been there. Because he was startled, he turned around and knocked me back off balance. It was nothing that a sorry couldn't fix, but it was a good example of not waiting and losing advantage, but rather if something catches you off-guard, react in measured ways to ensure you do not lose or give advantage to the other person. Most of us would wait until we were crystal clear as to what's going on. Doing this when someone surprises you and/or tries to attack you means you probably lost the battle, or at least gave them a huge advantage. Better to take some measured action, whether that is pushing the other person off-balance, or something as simple as turning your weak side toward the person and your strong gun side away from them, or gaining some distance between you and the other person. This can make all the difference.

Keep in mind that most bad guys use your civility against you. They use it to get in close or catch you off guard; you have to know when it's time to turn the politeness off. Don't wait until it's too late. I'd rather be impolite and deter the attack than be polite and end up having to shoot him. Boundaries help to keep us safe. Whether that boundary is distance, or a wall, or simply saying no, or through gunfire, if it comes to that.

One way you learn to think like a cop is to think like a criminal. Think, if you were a criminal, what would you do or what advantage would you be looking for, if for instance, you wanted to attack a lady? Would you look for a group of ladies and pick one out of the group where there's going be lots of witnesses, or would you rather wait until you see one lady by herself? Would you look for someone that is in good lighting and long sightlines where there is likely to be a witness, or would you rather look for someone in a confined area in low light where there is less likelihood of a witness standing by? A place where it would be difficult for you to get away if you needed to, or would you look for somewhere that you could flee easily and get on to a major road or freeway so you can disappear? If you were a bad guy, and we're looking for money, would you look for someone that looks like they've been wearing the same clothes for days, or would you look for us a snappy dresser with expensive clothes or jewelry? Would you look for someone larger or smaller than you, someone that you could overpower easily or someone that could put up a fight, someone with a tie-dyed shirt that says, "Thespians for peace", or someone with a baseball hat that says "DefenseSHOT" on it? Might your chances be better of overpowering someone driving a Prius with a "Coexist" sticker on it, or a car with a "Defense Shot alumni" sticker on it? This is one reason we offer the Defense Shot alumni stickers in our classes; they are friendly and subtle, but they get the point across that you are not likely to be a victim.

Think about sightlines whenever possible, the longer your sightlines (that is to say, the farther you can look in all directions) the better because it gives you more time to see what's coming and more time to react. Longer sightlines also mean that there will more likely be other witnesses that can see you from wherever they are standing. This is why I don't recommend parking between large vehicles for instance, if you were in a small car. It's not a great idea to park between two tall vans, or a couple of trucks; these are things that would block your view of what is around you as well as blocking the view of other would be witnesses from seeing you should you be attacked. Rather than parking between high profile vehicles, it might be a better option, even if it means parking further out, to park near shorter vehicles or no vehicles at all so your sightlines are greatly increased. Park near lights when possible. If you have a choice, park away from bushes. Think sightlines; let this be your guide as to where to park and where to walk. Distance is your friend.

Delinquents use two avenues of approach. The first one is to be subtle, or even seem friendly. These guys might use the approach of seeming helpful, like they are going to help you with your groceries, or your flat tire, while others tend to come in seeming like they need your help, such as asking for directions, or a handout. The intent is to close the distance between you and him so that you lose the advantage of distance. Maybe one of the most obvious examples of this in my past was standing out on Salt Lake Flats at the end of a dead-end road when a car pulled up and some people popped out of it looking around just as we were. The thing that was odd though was that one guy wanted to stand uncomfortably close to me the entire time. Maybe he was a close talker, but being that we could literally see miles and miles in every direction and he insisted on standing within a couple feet of me was unnerving. As a result, I tried to put distance between us whenever possible, kept my gun side away from him, and stayed ready. Also, my wife who had also noticed this, kept her distance from me so that we were not in the same direction of this guy. This way, if something did go wrong he would have problems coming from two different directions. Now he might have been nothing more than someone who likes to stand awkwardly close to people, but the actions that my wife and I took while unobtrusive, offered no advantage to him if he had turned out to have nefarious purposes. We'll never know whether this was a bad guy for certain, or just a close talker. Why? He was never offered a decent opportunity to strike. In other words, if he was a bad guy there was no opportunity of advantage offered him, so he wouldn't have attacked unless he was incredibly foolish.

This is another example where boundaries and not giving up tactical advantage can keep both you and the bad guy safe. The easiest battle to win is the one you never have to fight. Learning to watch your surroundings, which we call *situational awareness*, and keeping your tactical advantages often will keep you safe and out of harm's way in the first place. As it was, we were able to keep tactical advantage by separating. One of us standing behind an open car door would not look obvious to anyone unaware of our tactical position, but to someone looking for an advantage to attack, the opportunity was never given.

The next step, if it comes to this, after trying to position yourself, is the use of voice. This could be as simple as saying, *"Hey, you might want to step back; you don't want to get what I've got,"* insinuating that maybe you've got a cold, but don't be bashful about barking at someone and telling them to get away if you need to.

An attackers second avenue of approach is simply by surprise, or bold, overwhelming action. Many bad guys are learning what people in battle have known for a long time: action almost always beats reaction, meaning that if someone throws an unexpected sucker punch, it's almost certain to beat the reaction time of the other person trying to throw up an arm to block. Action beats reaction. These criminals tend to be very bold, march straight at you, and take action without any notice or other conversation. This is a little harder to counter subtly. Some of the telltale signs are people doing what I call the "swivel head". In other words, if someone gets out of their car or walks into the room, and swivels his head around, taking notice of everything in the room before wandering towards you, or marching toward you, that's a red flag. Those people are usually looking to see if there are other witnesses or cops before they close in for the attack.

The other thing to look for is someone walking toward you who looks like they're on a mission. Most people wander through life at a leisurely pace. If someone looks like they're walking as if they were late to work, but they're coming in your direction, that's another red flag. Now, we're not going to clear leather and shoot somebody simply for walking toward us, but we are going to take action to mitigate his or her advantage. This could be securing distance between you and the other person, or simply turning your gun side away and offering them your weak side. Even addressing them as they walk towards you, saying something like, "Hey! What do you want?" If you are not the intended target, you might notice the bad guy marching toward someone else. Again this gives you the opportunity to clear out, or respond in any other lawful way you see necessary.

I lost count of how many times on duty watching out for what I call "swivel heads" has paid off for me. Many times when I was on duty and in uniform, I would notice someone who kept staring in my direction every once in a while. This isn't normal. It was usually an indication of someone who was either feeling guilty about something, or looking for an opportunity to get away with something. Either way, noticing this paid off many, many times. Often it turned out to be someone who was guilty of a crime, or had a warrant out for his or her arrest, or was the lookout for someone else getting ready to commit a crime.

Remember, weapons usually come from the hand. This means you should keep an eye on where people's hands are. If someone's hand is slipped inside of a bag, or inside their jacket pocket, that should draw more attention than someone with hands dangling at their sides. Keep in mind that most weapons come from the waistband, so if you see someone fiddling around under their shirt, that should draw your attention. One way to tell if people are moving their hands without staring at their hands is to watch their shoulders. It's pretty hard to move your hands without telegraphing that move through the shoulders. If you're watching their head and shoulders, you'll usually notice their shoulders move, which will give you a heads up that their hands are moving. This is also why if you are ever in a situation where you are trading blows with someone, you don't watch the hands, you watch the shoulders for the telegraphed move. I learned and used this extensively in martial arts. It also offered me the extra time to get a block up and kept me from getting hit many times on duty.

Many levels of action can keep you from harm. These actions start small but can quickly escalate if necessary. You may also need to skip steps and go from 1 strait to 7 if need be. See the chart on the next page.

LEVELS OF ACTION AND USE OF FORCE ESCALATION

1. Command presence
2. Placement
3. Gestures and/or voice
4. Physical restraint or strikes
5. Less lethal force such as pepper spray if you have it
6. Producing you gun
7. Shooting
8. Using your vehicle as a weapon

Now, let's flesh out each of these levels.

1. *Command Presence*

   This means having a demeanor that does not look submissive, unsure or weak, which only invites attack. Look calm, confident, aware, and in control. If you have ever watched two people having lunch where one is the boss and the other is the employee, you can spot the difference. People give off constant subtle cues with body language, posture and gestures that indicate who is in charge and who is submissive. This does not mean looking mean, tough or abrasive. You can be happy or even silly and still look confident.

2. *Placement*

   Should you find your encounter with someone who seems like a possible threat, move and place yourself to a position of advantage. Often times that position may be in the next zip code. If there is no time to leave, move so there is an obstacle or cover between you and the suspect. If you must remain in the area in close proximity, move so that your gun and strong side are away from the suspect. Ideally, if you must be near him try to be behind him on his strong side. If you are out of time and think you may need to shoot, consider moving so that people are not behind your target if possible. This could include not only moving right and left but also squatting down so that the background behind his chest and head are more likely to be the ceiling. Also consider whether you need to

95

move so that people are not behind you if he returns fire.

3. *Gestures and/or Voice*
This includes yelling clear commands and pointing directions with your non-gun hand.

4. *Physical restraints or strikes*
When you are in close it may be necessary to block, grab or hit the person who is trying to seriously injure you. As a quick note, usually holds or pushes are more effective than strikes.

5. *Less Lethal Force: Pepper Spray Tasers and Stun Guns*
See Chapter: 4 "Extra Equipment: Pros and Cons" for further parameters.

6. *Unholstering your Gun*
It's important to understand that you must have the exact same threat criteria against you (eminent threat of great bodily injury) to shoot, as you need to unholster the gun in the first place. The only reason this is separated from level 7, "Shooting" is because in the vast majority of cases this level stops the threat and you are not forced to shoot (Thank God). However, it's important that you are prepared to shoot if necessary.

7. *Shooting*
You only shoot to stop the treat. The instant the treat stops, the gunfire stops.

8. *Vehicle*
Which has more force, your gun firing tiny metal projectiles weighing a fraction of an ounce at 1000 plus feet per second, or your 3000 pound car traveling 30 mph? It's important not to forget that all options are on the table if your life, or the lives of others, are clearly in eminent danger.

Officers will be judged on each of these levels, assuming they have all of the above tools and training. However, CCW carriers will usually not have pepper spray or be trained in restraint techniques, etc. The point here is to use the least amount of force to affect as safe an outcome as possible. For instance, if you can dissuade an attack from starting in the first place simply by your command presence—not looking like an easy victim, or by barking, *"Get away from me!"* then everyone goes home happy. Also, you would not be expected to use physical force (level 4) or pepper spray (level 5-) if you are outmatched, untrained, or the tools were not available to you. Extra tools are nice, but unless you are well trained, they can become a liability. It's no good having your hand full with a can of pepper spray only to realize you should have reached for your gun. Again, it's also important to realize that sometimes you have to go from level 1, *Command Presence* strait to 7, *Shooting*, if there is no time left to try the other steps.

Your presence and the way you carry yourself can stop problems often before they start. This does not mean being gruff all the time. If you have met me, I'm sure you'll find me quite approachable. The *tough guy* front, the person who insists on looking puffed up all the time, is usually a pushover and using the puffed up persona as a defense mechanism, although not a very good one. The puffed up tough guy or tough gal persona causes more problems than it can ever dissuade.

What we are looking to project is calm, friendly confidence. Think Chuck Norris, not Hulk Hogan. Should it come time for you to get serious, whether that means barking orders or clearing your holster, think calculated, prepared, professional, stepping in to fix the problem. Not crazy, out of control person who is losing their mind.

I have found over the years, most bad guys don't respect you if you seem like you're out of control, or using bad language. I suspect this is because everyone these bag guys are around talks to them and acts like this; you're probably using the same language that his mother does, so it does not impress him at all. What does appear to be effective is seeming professional, using clear, loud commands and not adding any words that you would not want read back to a jury in court. Coming across direct, loud and professional usually has a better response. The bad guy tends to take you more seriously.

— Chapter 11 —

LETTER OF THE LAW VS
SPIRIT OF THE LAW

AN IMPORTANT DISTINCTION TO APPRECIATE IS THE DIFFERENCE between the letter of the law and the spirit of the law. The spirit focuses on what the intent of the law is, whereas the letter focuses on crossing every *t* and dotting every *i*. A good example of this when it comes to guns is the federal law regarding the transport of handguns in vehicles. The letter of the law in part states that any handgun (that you don't have covered by your CCW) must be locked in a container. The ammunition cannot be in the container with the gun or near the container. Clearly the spirit of the law here is to make sure that people aren't driving around with an unloaded handgun sitting on the passenger seat and the ammunition right next to it so that they can load up at a moment's notice.

When you buy a gun usually the gun store provides a cheap cable lock designed to be threaded through the gun and then locked in such a way that the gun cannot be loaded or operated. This gets it out the door or the gun store legally, but it does not get it into your vehicle legally. If you were to take the gun and place this cable lock through the gun and then transport that gun in a vehicle—lets say behind the back seat—with the ammunition in the front floorboard, you would not be legal when checked against the letter of the law because the letter of the law specifically states that the gun must be in a locked container. However if you were to take the cable lock off of that gun and wrap it around the handle of the clamshell style plastic box the gun typically comes in, you would now have a locked container. So let's ask ourselves the question: which way was the gun actually more secured? Clearly it's more secure to have the cable lock through the gun because it would be harder to break the cable lock than it would be to break the plastic box open.

Before we continue, allow me to reiterate that I am very pro-Peace Officer. I was one for my entire career and so was my father who co-instructs with me. You will find very few people more pro-cop. Having said that, cops are humans not robots. So there will be anomalies from time to time. Okay let's continue. If you transported your gun with a cable lock through the gun as described above and you got pulled over—depending on what area of the country you're in and what city you're in—most cops would be fine with the cable through the gun and ammunition transported as described above because you have complied with the spirit of the law. However, if you run into the few cops that want to go by the letter of the law rather than the spirit of the law, they would have cause to bust you. Now the likelihood that the district attorney would file on that case would be slim—again depending on what city or state you're in—but it has happened based on the letter of the law. If you are in a, let's call it "red" area you'd probably be fine, but if you found yourself in a "blue" area of the country, you'd be more likely to have a problem with the district attorney filing on that case. But even if the district attorney doesn't file on you in this case, you have beaten the rap but you still did not beat the ride. In other words, you could find yourself arrested for something and then waiting until the district attorney looks at the case and dismisses it. Regardless of where you are, it's important to understand not only the spirit of the law (the intent of the law), but also the letter of the law. You want to be following the letter of the law not only because it keeps you legal, but also in case you run into an officer that doesn't understand the difference.

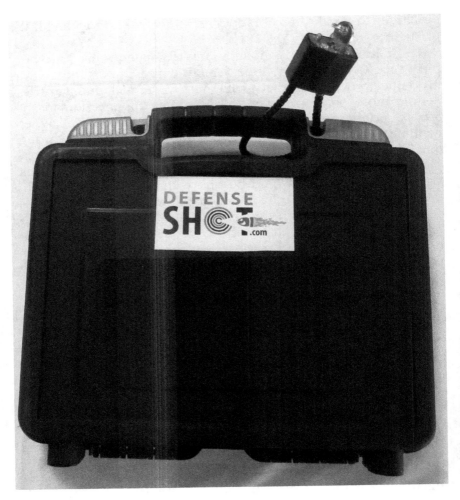

Now let's cover legislation on the fly. Once in a great while you'll find someone who's just making rules up as they go along. This is far less common than those insisting on the letter of the law. To give you a non-law-enforcement example, recently I was in a large box store. Standing just ahead of me in line was a nice couple—clearly in their thirties—buying some beer. The goofball running the cash register suddenly stopped while processing their sale and stated that he needed to see the identification of both people. The gentleman who was actually purchasing the beer with his ATM card had his identification on him and produced it to prove that he was over 21. His wife, who was not purchasing the beer, did not have her wallet on her, so the cashier held up the line while she walked all the way out to the parking lot to retrieve her ID and return. While she was walking out, I had a polite conversation with the cashier. I explained to him that demanding ID from everyone in the party purchasing the beer was not required by law, nor was it logical. I asked him if the couple in question had had children with them, would he require them to produce identification for him too? Would he have refused to sell the beer to the adult with the ID if he had a child in tow? Even though this guy was clearly getting the bigger picture, he stuck by his guns to protect his pride by stated, "Well, it's really complicated... They make me do that." He was off to blaming the fictional "they" for a rule he just made up on the cusp. In the off chance that you run into an officer like this, it's usually better to go along to get along at the time, and then fix it later by filing a complaint unless you really understand the law and are able to clarify without escalating the situation. After all, if this person is willing to make up their own rules, they may also be willing to make up their own facts later.

Some may think I'm jaded for this way of thinking, but actually I'm being pragmatic. I've seen it happen before not only with rookies, but also with a supervisor who I was forced to correct on the spot in front of the suspect before things spiraled out of control. If a person like this has extreme confirmation bias they may really be convinced that they saw you do or heard you say something differently than what actually transpired, especially later while writing a report. Here is an example of confirmation bias in every day life: what happens if a ball is very close to the line on a game-ending call? One team will insist the ball was in, and the other team will be emphatic it was out. To say that we are going to go along to get along at the time is not to say that we are going to give up our rights to someone, but it's important to pick the time and place to correct the situation.

These types of people are very few and far between in what most would consider mainstream law enforcement such as sheriff's departments and police departments, but they are just a little bit more common in ancillary officer positions like park rangers, game wardens and others. As an example, the El Dorado County Sheriff in California (a very pro-gun Sheriff) recently had to take the badge away from a ranger who was working in the national forest in the county for repeatedly harassing people. And it wasn't as though the sheriff hadn't given warnings to him and his agency ahead of time. I can guarantee you that this type of person when not legislating on the fly, is also the kind of person that will want to go by the strictest letter of the law. This is one reason it's important to know the letter of the law and not just the spirit of the law. If we're going by the letter of the law, we're going to avoid a lot of potential headaches. Remember that ignorance of the law is not usually seen as a viable excuse, unless you're a former attorney, turned senator, turned presidential nominee or something like that, just as a random example.

Staying current with laws is important. Signing up to receive our DefenseSHOT.com bi-monthly updates on your email or text, will help keep you abreast of the situation as well as give you new tips on shooting and carrying and discounts we find. What you will not receive on these updates is every proposed change or negotiation; those are so common and vacillate so much they are just confusing. I'll spare you that. On our updates you'll receive information on what actually *becomes* law, not all the rumors and negotiations in between. The only exceptions I make to that rule are when I see proposed legislation that will cause a run on the guns and ammunition, which happens from time to time. When I see those, I'll give you a heads up in time to beat the rush and the associated price increases on those items. My track record on that has been so accurate that gun stores follow me for my advice on market demand.

— Chapter 12 —

WHAT TO SAY TO OFFICERS IN DIFFERENT SITUATIONS

I LOVE COPS. It's silly that I have to point this out, but I do because some people take this information wrong. My father and co-CCW Instructor was a cop. I was a cop. I am very pro-cop; you won't find too many people more pro-cop than me.

Cops are friends and we love to be able to talk to them under all circumstances to explain what transpired, but if you just injured somebody, you can't do that and here's why. Everything you say can and will be used against you in a court of law. Some ambulance-chaser attorney will find the bad guy you injured, or his family, and try to make money off of you. They'll come back in the court with some lawsuit claiming that the guy you shot was the greatest guy ever, and now they want to get paid. Anything and everything that you said to the officers can be documented. The ambulance-chasing attorney will get a hold of those documents and twist every word you said to make you lose credibility. For instance, you may say something while you're upset and in the heat of the moment to the cops like, "Yes, I was forced to shoot that dirt bag." Well the first part of that sentence worked out great, but the second part is going to cost you a lot of money, because the attorney is going to use that to insinuate that you had animus towards the person you shot. He'll insist that it wasn't that your life was an eminent danger. He'll insist that the fact that you didn't like the guy was the reason you shot, and clearly you hated him because you called him a *dirt bag*. The attorney will insist you weren't in

103

danger at all, but because of your bigoted view, you were scared for no reason. And heaven forbid the assailants social status, skin color, or religion is different than yours. Otherwise we could turn this whole thing into a three-ring circus with the media. They will be happy to pass judgment and hang you in the court of public opinion.

**Father & Son on duty together
'92**

Here's another factor. We've all had the experience of thinking we said one thing but sometimes the words spoken are slightly different than our intention. I've done this during some my CCW classes. I may talk for 10 hours straight during the day since I really don't get breaks. The brakes are times for people to come up and ask questions. During one of these days it's common for me to say one thing while thinking I said another. Once in a while I have even thrown a "not" in the middle of what should be a positive statement, completely reversing the intended idea. Usually this sticks out like a sore thumb and people realize what I meant, but that's also one reason that my co-instructor is in the back waving at me once in a while.

One of my *Johnisms* is to say, "I know what I'm talking about; I just don't know what I'm saying." I'm not the only one doing this, in fact there are couples I know that, if filmed, could make a fantastic reality show. You can hear one saying one thing and the spouse hearing something completely different; it's great comedy.

If you've ever watched a political talk show with two people from opposite sides of the aisle, you know exactly what I'm talking about. I'm not sure if they're intending to hear things wrong, or if they really have that much confirmation bias that anything they hear from the opposing side must be wrong and reinterpreted. Now, instead of having the spouse on a different wavelength, or the talk show host holding an opposing view, try having your statements interpreted by an ambulance-chasing attorney who is actively intending to hear things in a way that makes him money. How do you think that's going to go over? What if the district attorney is suspicious of you because of other statements made by witnesses who saw something different than your observation? And now because of the suspicion, the judge or jury is going over every statement you made with a fine toothcomb to see if what you did was actually criminal?

Assume every word you say to the officer is documented. Also, it's safe to assume that every word you say to the officer that is documented will be misused against you. On second thought, don't assume it, you can almost guarantee it, that's why it's in your Miranda Rights—you know the statement: *"Anything you say can and will be used against you in a court of law..."* That doesn't sound like a warning, it sounds like a promise, doesn't it? That means every word you said could be arming an attorney, even answering a question with a simple, "I don't know" could harm you.

On top of that, if you have already started answering questions and then suddenly refuse to answer a question; that could hurt you. It's not hard to imagine a scenario where the cops get there and you're happy to answer their questions because you've done nothing wrong, and you're so relieved they're there to help you until you hear a question that you think might be probing at criminal intent, or could easily be misconstrued, and so you choose not to answer. Or you say, "Maybe I should talk to an attorney." As soon as you do that, the officer is going to note the question that he asked and the fact that you refused to answer that question after formerly being quite open. The district attorney and/or the ambulance-chasing attorney will speak of this in conspiratorial tones. Since you were quite willing to talk until you heard the all-important question, the question that would've proven that you were a bad guy, and then suddenly you clammed up.

Conversely, when the cop showed up if you had simply said, " I want to talk to my attorney," at that point, before the questioning started, the fact that you asked for an attorney *cannot* be used against you in court. It cannot even be mentioned. But make the mistake of waiting until after you've answered a question or two and then trying to invoke that right, then it becomes fair game in court that you asked for an attorney.

But wait it gets worse. Even if you said everything perfectly and your statements would help your case, you were talking to an officer who is a human being, and a human being is not infallible. This means there's a possibility some of the things you said will be misunderstood or mistranscribed when the officer is taking notes, or when hours later he looks at his notes while writing his report— hey, we're all human. But guess what? When the officer's report doesn't match your statement, you will be seen as the liar. The officer will be seen as an impartial trained observer. The officer doesn't have a reason to change his statements but you may since you *may* be trying to hide something. This is the way it will be seen.

Often officers are working double-shifts. It's very common to be working a 16-hour shift. Do you know the cognitive ability of someone after 16 hours of work? Many employers have done studies on this; after eight hours of work you're pretty much through. By 10 hours, you're almost worthless in most industries. As an example, your driving skills at that point are somewhere on par with someone who's had a few drinks. So it's not inconceivable that you might make a statement indicating that you screamed, "I have a gun. I don't want to shoot you," but the officer hours later writes in his report that you said "I have a gun; I'll shoot you." Things like this become problematic to say the least. Maybe you told him you fired five shots and he wrote down that you stated you fired three shots. But the physical evidence shows that there were five cases on the ground and five bullets were recovered later. Guess who's a big fat liar? You are. People usually assume the officer is impartial, trained and almost infallible. What he said is likely to be taken as the gospel truth so when his report doesn't match your statement, they'll assume you must've lied and there begins your misfortune.

Now at this point we only covered what *might* happen if the officer misinterprets what he heard you say, that's only half of the equation because he's also going to write down the questions that he asked you. He may have asked you the question slightly differently than he thought he was asking. He may recount the question slightly differently than he asked. In this case, even if you answered his question perfectly, if his question changes from the time it comes out of his mouth to the time he puts it on paper, this could also cause confusion or misrepresentation of your responses. Not to mention the likelihood of you misunderstanding a question because of the stress and then answering the question based on your confusion.

If you are forced to injure somebody to save yourself or someone else from the eminent danger of death or great bodily injury, please consider saying the following: " I was in fear for my life; I want my attorney." If you want to add the cherry on top you could say, "Thank God you're here" or "I'm so glad you're here." Why do we say this? Every cop in the nation has been told that if they have to use their gun they are to make the same statement, "I was in fear for my life. I want my attorney and my union rep." The officer will have 24 hours, or in some cases even more time before submitting a statement. You're going to say the same thing, except you don't get a union rep.

Saying *I was in fear for my life; I want my attorney* takes care of several things. First off, when you say this to the cop, he's going to have a Pavlovian response; he's going to think that's exactly what I would say. Which in a way, on some level, is likely to put him on your side. You've also provided him all the information he needs to precede. You've indicated that you were the victim, the other person was trying to take your life or someone else's life, and that you will not be making any further statements because you're smart. Not guilty, smart.

Many people don't take advantage of their right not to speak without the attorney present because they've been brainwashed. We all watched cop shows for decades and in every show only the bad guys lawyer up. You've been conditioned to think that only bad guys need rights. You see how silly it is when you hear it that way? *Only bad guys need rights?* I'll admit that even I have used the browbeating technique or awkward silence allowing the other person to assume that they should be able to talk to me if they've have nothing to hide. It's simply a method that we use to get more information. Even though I may have furrowed my brows in an attempt to get more information, the reality is I tell my family that if they are ever in an investigation, they are never to answer questions. This is the same advice my dad, who is also a cop and a detective, gave me.

Many people think that if they blab enough they won't have to wear the chrome bracelets and take a ride to booking. This is not true. When I rolled up on a scene, I made my decision whether the suspect was taking a ride in the patrol car based on what I saw and maybe the statements of individuals who were not involved in the incident. I didn't believe a word that the possible suspect said anyways, so if he said something that would bolster his case, I'd probably assume he was lying. If you are the possible suspect, nothing you can say will keep you from taking a ride to booking. I have never had a case where I rolled up on the scene and thought that guys going to jail and then have the suspect talk me out of taking him in. It's not going to happen. What will happen is that everything you say can and will be used against you if not by the district attorney then by the ambulance-chasing attorney who is going to try to take your money. The conversation you have with the officer while you're trying to get your way clear of a ride to booking will be the most expensive conversation you ever had, so don't have it. If the officer is smart, he's not going to let your statements keep you from taking a ride.

John Sr. 1993
Served from late
60's - early 2000's

It's just best to assume that you're going to take a ride. Maybe you won't if there's enough physical evidence on scene that indicates what happened or enough uninvolved strangers who were witnesses, but your testimony will not change the officer's mind as to what happened, so don't try. You'll only hurt your case and spend sleepless months wondering what questions were asked, what you said, how you were perceived, and how it was recorded or reported.

Assume that the bad guy's family members see you as their next lotto ticket. Here's an example and let's just claim it's hypothetical. Hypothetically, I may have had a partner years ago who ended up shooting a guy who had spent years in prison and had not seen his family for many, many years. The reason he had been in prison was for beating down his mother so bad that he nearly killed her. His family never talked to him after that. Now, hypothetically, when my partner had to shoot the guy, guess who showed up with an attorney claiming that, the decedent was their favorite son and how wonderful he was and how much they missed him? Hypothetically speaking of course.

— Chapter 13 —

THE THIN VEIL OF CIVILITY

YEARS AGO THERE WAS A FAMOUS WEALTHY MAN who went bankrupt. He was asked how it happened. How did he lose it all? His answer was basically, "Very gradually at first, and then all of the sudden." The stories you see in the newspaper are only a tiny fraction of the crimes that are committed each day. Often the ones reported aren't even the most heinous. My father, and co-author, was a cop for over 35 years. He was also a Sheriff's Detective, Inspector, and Deputy Coroner. He investigated everything from Internal Investigations, to homicides, kidnappings, and crimes against children—to put it mildly. He says people are capable of such monstrosity and cruelty that horror movies can't even come close. Humans are capable of being more vicious and cruel than any animal on the planet. As a kid, I remember my dad saying that if people had any idea what was going on around them each day, they would never leave their house. Since then it's becoming worse. Even to the point that watching the tiny sliver of sanitized highly edited version of reality that we see on the TV news is making it obvious that the wheels of society are wobbling. The veneer of civility is very thin.

THE SHEEP
Society has become increasingly narcissistic. People are not genuinely interested in one another. You've probably noticed this even in something as innocent as customer service. I spend about 30% of my time now cleaning up after other people's incompetence in the service sector, despite the fact that I'm paying for their service. This used to be common when dealing with a government agency, but now it's even stretched into the private sector. So many people these days just don't care what

happens to anyone around them. You've probably noticed on TV, when someone is getting attacked and the other people are standing around filming it with their phones! Why are they doing this? One explanation is people aren't willing to take the risk of getting injured themselves. A second reason is that they have been programmed to believe they shouldn't get involved. This one is especially true with the younger crowd who had 12 years of training to be sheep. Trained that if they got involved, often they were meted out the same punishment as the aggressor. A third reason is because they're concerned about capturing good film and taking credit for it, rather than stepping in and helping. I've even seen cases where four or five people are standing around filming and watching while one person pummels the other into the pavement. Those four or five people standing around—even if weaker or disabled—are probably capable of stopping the bad guy simply by the sheer numbers available. Heck, if those people had put their phones down and simply went over to sit on the bad guy, that would be the end of the problem in some cases.

How were a few guys with box cutters reportedly able to overpower an entire airliner full of people? Really that shouldn't even be possible with a gun. So how is it plausible? It's plausible because so many people freeze up, or turn their backs to run because they think someone else will take care of the problem or they can wait it out. So many of these attacks could quickly be resolved with far less loss of life if we could only change the average person's mindset. On duty, if a few of us decided to subdue a suspect and pin him to the ground, we called it a "pig pile." A pig pile doesn't require skill, just weight. These are some examples of defense being each individual's responsibility that cannot be delegated to others.

THE WOLVES

What happens to society when the lights go out—so to speak? What happens to a society that is fed a pervasive diet of violence and sex as entertainment, a society that exalts self-indulgence and perversion and actively denigrates dignity and self-restraint as stuffy, old, and even hateful, when the lights go out?

The wheels come off within hours. That's what happens. The first victims are those who are seen as easy targets of opportunity. The next victims are women and girls. Things only continue downhill from there. This happened during

112

hurricane Katrina, the L.A. riots, when New Jersey was hit by a storm, and on and on. The crime comes in waves. The first to take part are the opportunist criminals. Those who are always looking to get away with whatever they can. When people like this realize the cops are busy, they immediately start looting. Within hours, these people are emboldened as they see they can get away with anything. That's when they start attacking women and girls, and anyone who gets in the way of that attack. It doesn't take long for them to realize that if they can distract emergency services further, they can be even more brazen so they start to set things on fire and complete chaos ensues. To make things worse, organized gangs spring into action as a group.

Using a group to accomplish any task is a force multiplier. In other words, five bad guys working together are going to cause far more than five times the damage, with relative impunity. Once bad guys gang up, they don't even need weapons to be able to take anything or anyone they want by force from those who are unarmed, under armed and untrained. If a few home invaders kick your door in to take your stuff, do you think they are going to overlook your wife or daughter? Or you? Consider that. Now consider your loved ones. You owe it to each of them and to yourself to be armed and trained to our DefenseSHOT Advanced shooting level.

In San Jose, known as Silicon Valley, an affluent city in the Bay Area of California, a few years back there was a power outage that only lasted a matter of hours. The power went out mid-day. By that evening, even "normal" respectable people were beginning to get tense, and while trying to keep it hidden, starting to assume an "every man for himself" mentality as they realized it would soon be dark. People began hoarding water, nonperishable food, and other supplies. Tempers started to flair as others who also didn't have preparations came to the stores to try to stock up. (Note: the time to prepare has already passed at this point. You need to be prepared ahead of time, or you may as well forget it. Trying to prepare after the fact is putting yourself in danger.) Criminals began to test the waters by shoplifting en mass. Five finger discounts were everywhere on small items, no doubt these people were chomping at the bit for the sun to go down so things could really get rolling. Thankfully, the power came back on as it got dark. If it hadn't, the nice city would have been off the rails by morning.

A MOST LIKELY THREAT

On April 16, 2013, a PG&E electrical sub-station at Metcalf in Coyote, California was attacked. A man, or men fired AK-47s at 17 transformers, which caused the oil to escape thereby causing the transformers to overheat, which shut down the substation. This was considered by Homeland Security to be a sophisticated attack and they suspect there was an insider. It shut down power in the area including the TRUNK system – which is the communications system for law enforcement, fire and EMS radios and communication which effected law enforcement's ability to coordinate or even disseminate information to their own staff. Power was redirected from another substation to cover the resulting outage until 15 million dollars in reconstruction could be accomplished.

I remember hearing about it on the news. They made it sound as if some simpletons had used it for target practice. I also remember thinking their coverage was garbage; it was. Turns out this was a sophisticated attack complete with directed wave lights to confuse the security cameras and other measures taken to avoid shedding evidence. Here's what concerns those of us with law enforcement or military backgrounds: this was absolutely without question what is known as "a dry run." It was a test, a proof of concept, proof that a portion of the electrical grid can be taken down with $40 worth of common ammunition. And if the person doesn't mind being caught, it doesn't even have to be sophisticated.

Here's the bigger problem. If as few as six or eight other stations are taken out at the same time, it will cause a cascade effect taking down most of the United States and the outage could last for months. The power grid needs other parts of itself in order to jumpstart. If the jumper cables are missing—other substations down—there's no way to jumpstart it. Add to that, many of the necessary parts aren't made in America. They are only made in China. I have had face-to-face meetings with FEMA employees who flatly state they expect if or when the grid were to go down for anything close to a year, the national fatality rate would be in the ballpark of 90 plus percent. Why, because of lack of medical facilities? That's a small fraction. Would it be due to a lack of clean food, water and sanitation? That's a bigger piece of the pie. The biggest problem would be civil unrest. FEMA realizes that if the lights go out, the thin veil of civility will evaporate very quickly. Only one in ten would be left after less than twelve months.

Clearly someone funded this dry run on Coyote Canyon for a reason. No doubt whoever did so wanted proof of concept so they could confidently attack anytime in the future, if or when they choose. This was certainly the work of a terrorist group or even another government. Worse yet, any group or entity that paid attention is also now aware that they can do the same. Most people think it would take a nuke or bioweapon to eviscerate America. Wrong. It would take a handful of bad guys—who don't even need specialized training—at a few substations on the same day. So why not guard the substations? There are thousands of substations that could be targeted. Any group or government can simply attack them and then stand back and let America tear itself apart. And the chaos would likely cover the tracks or give plausible deniability to the entity that caused the attack which is another plus for this approach.

The veneer of civility is very thin no matter where you are. People who believe they are immune because they don't live in a "bad area" are fooling themselves. Bad people are mobile and problems spread quickly. As an example, if the Bay Area has a catastrophic event—a major earthquake, a prolonged power outage, a bioterror attack, or a multitude of other problems that would cause the densely inhabited area to implode—the busiest corridor in the country will be Interstate 80 running east out of the Bay Area according to FEMA. As those roads come to a standstill—which they will—it's projected that people will abandon their vehicles and affect all areas within six miles of the highway in both directions, as well as the surrounding areas of all secondary routes and roads. The same scenario could play out near any city.

After the common criminals and the gangs—keeping in mind that we are talking about not only established street gangs but also impromptu gangs—the next group to become uncivil are the desperate: those who under normal circumstances would be law-abiding. Many of these people just need a reason or a push. The same people who are willing to go without food for themselves or their spouse may be willing to attack others to feed their kids for instance. In Venezuela as the government collapsed to communism in 2017, and food became scarce, first the pets disappeared, then the pigeons. Many of the first people targeted and murdered were cops. People wanting to protect their families or their group targeted law enforcement. People were suddenly doing, what to them was unthinkable only a day before, murdering a cop to take his gun so that they could protect themselves from others in what they perceive to be an "every man for himself" scenario.

I mention the above for two reasons. First, to focus a spotlight on how thin the veneer of civility is, and how easily it is peeled away. In collective cases, it happens in times of crisis, however individually—one person or a small group attacking—can be instigated simply by the appearance of an opportunity, or sparked by an unreasonable person having a difficult time. It doesn't take much. There doesn't have to be a catastrophic event for you to get attacked. Your life could end simply because you cut off an unstable person having a bad day and you cutting him off accidently was the last straw.

The second reason I bring this to your attention is that the only time to prepare for any event is *before* it happens. Failing to prepare is preparing to fail. This means getting your CCW, and training in our Defense and Advance Defense Shooting classes so you and those you care about are not victims. We offer private, discreet classes and consultations and also offer an AR-15 rifle course as well. Feel free to contact me directly. The money I'll save you on your purchases of storable food alone will more than pay for the consultation. What I do is not some zany nonsense that you might see on a cable channel or simply buying a bunch of toys you will never use. We cover responsible, realistic plans for contingencies. When something goes wrong, the last place you want to be is in line trying to get supplies. That is one of the most vulnerable situations in which to find yourself. Starting this year many banks have bug-in bags in case they need to stay there for days. They aren't doing this out of paranoia. The threat concern is based on expert research.

Today, stores don't even have a backroom supply. Most big name stores receive five to six truck deliveries a day. Years ago, the shelves were stocked. Nowadays there's not much behind the first few items on the shelf, and no storeroom in the back of a modern store. This is called "just in time delivery". As the item is scanned at the register, a new one is loaded on the truck to be delivered. How long do you think the shelves will have items on them if the trucks don't arrive? Now exacerbate the problem by increasing perceived necessity—and as a result—demand for those items by about 1000%. It makes the worst actors fighting and trampling each other at a Black Friday event look tame. Even if you secure the items you will likely be targeted as you leave.

You need to plan ahead, train up, team up, and stock up beforehand. Also, people who have simply missed a few paychecks have a far less stressful time when they had stored foods. This is not Military MREs; I'm talking about the good stuff that you can serve and enjoy as a regular meal. You have car insurance, fire insurance, and savings for a rainy day; more than half the country doesn't even have a savings account by the way—that should concern you. You even have a gun just in case you are attacked. Why not have insurance in the form of training and provisions for a disaster or civil unrest? It's just another part of being responsible so that you can be part of a solution, rather than part of a problem. Or at least, so you and yours can safely sit things out for a few days, or weeks, or whatever is necessary. Like the examples of people I mentioned earlier, ignoring threats or assuming others will fix them only puts people at further risk. You owe it to yourself and your loved ones to be trained, because whether we are talking about one nut, or a small group of bad guys, or distraught masses, the veil of civility is incredibly thin.

— Chapter 14 —

CRAZY THOUGHTS AND
RIGHT BRAIN SHOOTING

IT'S FASCINATING WHAT KIND OF SCATTERBRAINED IDEAS COME into your head when you're under extreme pressure. I had a partner who had to hold a home invader at gunpoint in his own home. The night before we had worked the graveyard shift. He had gone home, put earplugs in, covered his eyes, and fell asleep. His wife got up later and went downstairs to the kitchen to do dishes. When she got to the sink, she looked out the window and saw a man standing outside the window staring directly at her. She screamed and instead of running away, he took a large pipe, broke the window and climbed in over the sink as she ran back upstairs to her husband. She shook him to wake him up. He didn't know what was going on, but understood there was a problem so he grabbed his gun and headed out into the hallway. He ended up meeting the intruder at the top of their stairs. The home invader, who was clearly there in order to attack his wife, was met face-to-face with my partner and his gun. He stood there and refused to leave, even though he was confronted at gunpoint. He kept lunging slightly towards my partner and clearly was looking for an opportunity to attack. This continued until the on-duty cops arrived and arrested the man. We all know exactly how this would've ended had he not been home, armed and trained.

The interesting factor in this case were the thoughts going through my partner's head during the ordeal. Musings such as the following arose, *"Geez, I just put this white carpet in and it's going to be ruined,"* and, *"If I have to shoot this guy and he dies, I'll have to let the realtors know if I decide to sell the house in the next couple of years.*" You'll have all kinds of unnecessary thoughts crowding your mind and you'll have trouble seeing all the small movements, facial expressions, and other indicators that require your attention. Not to mention the cognitive requirements of shooting: making a smooth trigger press, holding the gun steady, using your sights, using the correct shooting form for the situation, etc. Now, to add insult to injury, this incident ended up in the local paper mentioning my partner's name, where he was employed as an officer, and his home address in the article for all of our—let's call them clients—to see. As a result of the unwarranted broadcast, he did end up having to sell the house and move to a different town.

This case is a perfect illustration of the trivial notions that crowd your head when you're under extreme stress, the exact moment you don't have the luxury of time for other incidentals. This is precisely why it's imperative that you train with us, and commit your shooting abilities to your subconscious, so that you can do them correctly even under duress. Think of it this way, when you first learn to drive you had to actively think about putting your foot on the long skinny pedal to go, and to the fat pedal to slow down. You had to consciously consider which stick activates the turn signal and which the windshield wipers. Once you've practiced those skills again and again, they become committed to your subconscious. As a result, your ability to do those myriad movements under pressure is seamless and accurate, and they are accomplished in a fraction of the time compared to when you had to actively think about each and every action. This is because you have committed these actions to your subconscious. Now when you drive if something jumps out in front of you, you don't have to think *fat pedal slowdown* you just automatically break. Your reaction speed is a tiny fraction of what it used to be because your subconscious is hundreds of times faster than your conscious, analytical mind. When was the last time you consciously thought about the gas or brake?

We offer the same benefit for your shooting abilities; we very quickly move them from your conscious, analytical mind to your right brain or subconscious, so that they are accomplished without actively thinking about what you're

120

doing.   It's extremely critical to learn because if you're shooting abilities are in your conscious, analytical mind they will fall apart under pressure.   You'll end up spraying and praying and not hitting anything.   Whereas when it's in your subconscious, your motions become second nature, even under pressure.   Using traditional training methods, you could take many, many classes, and go through cases upon cases of ammo to push your shooting skills into your subconscious. Even then there are problems with such a shooting style because it tends to rely on fine motor skill.   Fine motor skills are absolutely unavailable when you are scared.   Traditional firearms training will leave you hanging out to dry in a stressful situation; however, using our method, we will instill the skillsets in your right brain, and train you to shoot accurately using gross motor skill only.   This is accomplished in a matter of hours, with far less expense and ammo fired. Not only does your shooting improve in speed, smoothness, and accuracy, but it will also work when you're so scared that you're thinking about the carpet or your next real estate transaction while someone's trying to attack you.

— Chapter 15 —

DON'T ASSUME YOU CAN REASON
WITH CRAZY PEOPLE

OFTEN CRAZY PEOPLE CAN'T BE REASONED WITH; however, most of them still respond to force. Unfortunately, sometimes we have to resort to that force. Let me give you an example. I interviewed a man who was spending a lengthy stay in a gated community, a.k.a. prison. The inmate had tried to rob somebody for his wallet. When the person didn't give him the wallet, he shot and killed the victim. Here's where it gets interesting: this inmate is still adamant that the judge and jury made the wrong decision. He insists the deceased man ought to be the one in prison. How did he rationalize this? In this idiot's words, he pointed a gun at the guy and told him, "Give me your wallet or I will shoot!" The guy did not give his wallet away so this idiot shot him. Even though he has been through court with all of the evidence presented against him, he continues to view himself as the victim. This crazy nut is not one of a kind; there are countless others like him. Do you think if this man or someone like him is holding a gun pointed at you and saying, *"Give me your wallet!"* there is any way to reason with him? It's nice to be able to talk people down when they're all amped up and getting ready to do something stupid, and most of the time this works, but there are situations where people just cannot be reasoned with.

One limitation inhibiting the ability to reason with crazy people is time. Do you have time to reason with this person, or talk them down before they do something violent? Often the answer is no. Second, you may not be able to reason with this person because of their lack of IQ, or decreased mental state due to intoxication. Third, you may not be able to reason with them because they have been brainwashed. Unfortunately, this last one has become far more common.

Our society has become one that flaunts victimhood. Everyone is encouraged to figure out how he is a victim of others, or of circumstances or a race and then identify with that victimhood. This is incredibly dangerous. People who buy into this nonsense tend to feel that they have been wronged and so anything they do to improve their position is fair game. In their mind, the end justifies the means. At any rate, the people who see themselves as the victim have somehow convinced themselves that anything they do to victimize others is not immoral, it's just fighting back. It's difficult to reason with people in this mindset. This is one reason why many people get attacked out of the blue without pretext: no argument, no disagreement, and no exchanged bad glances. It's situations like this that usually don't give you the chance to negotiate, or talk somebody down. These situations have always existed, but now it's becoming far more prevalent. The knock out game is an example. Randomly knocking out white people because; racism. (How ironic) Many times victims who identify with their perceived victimhood, instead of overcoming it, go on to continually victimize others.

— Chapter 16 —

A TRIAL ATTORNEY'S POINT OF VIEW

Living and acting in a manner that best prepares you to justify or defend the decision to stop a threat using lethal force possibly resulting in loss of life..

By: Michael Wise

THE DECISION TO ARM YOURSELF IS A DYNAMIC ELECTION. When you choose to be an armed American, you have taken a step that in many ways is irreversible and fraught with severe consequences. The obvious consequences entail the potential liability—both criminal and civil—if you are subsequently determined to not be justified or excused in your use of lethal force in that critical moment.

I have prosecuted and defended thousands of life-altering decisions, some of which were legally defensible choices, and many of which were not. Louis Pasteur taught us that, "chance favors the prepared mind." That statement applies to life in general, but is truly insightful for armed Americans who have chosen to accept the responsibility of affirmatively arming themselves, rather than being a victim to random or even deliberate violence. As a trial attorney, I often look to what is called *corroborative* or *indirect evidence* to establish a case for my clients. I frequently remind jurors in criminal cases that life corroborates itself daily; much like a stone tossed into a body of water creates ripples of affirmation, confirming infinitely that the stone broke the surface of the lake.

If you shoot someone and either strike the intended person, another person or no one at all; you will very quickly find yourself, your lifestyle, your social media, your communications and even your clothes, home décor and weapon choice under severe and even microscopic scrutiny. Very few people, no one in my experience, truly understand the invasive and stressful nature of litigation until they have endured that marathon of pain. This is even more true in criminal litigation, where you stand to lose not only your assets, money, and reputation, but also your freedom and in certain limited circumstances, your life.

Many people think they know how a criminal investigation unfolds. They watch television shows and movies depicting dramatic and heroic acts which are exciting. They see law enforcement officers engage in dramatic and illogical investigations, which magically produce plot-twisting results in an allotted amount of time. All the characters, whether portrayed as evil or good, are confident, self-assured and witty. Real life litigation is much less exciting, and tremendously draining for the average person. If you are fortunate enough to be out of custody while defending a serious criminal allegation, you will most often still find yourself unemployed, broke, ostracized, and depressed. If you are not so fortunate, you will find yourself sleeping on a 2-inch pad of foam, on a concrete bed, in a 10 x 10 cell with a roommate and only one hour a day of "recreation", which means access to telephones and a television that is shared with several other inmates sitting at metal tables in a larger concrete "common area." Neither option is glamorous or enticing.

Having defended several homicide cases, I have learned a lot about which aspects of daily life become relevant to a criminal investigation and prosecution. I've investigated and received government reports of those corroborative "ripples" within clients' lives that both sides review in their effort to present their case to a judge or jury seeking to secure "justice" as they define it at that moment.

When you are under criminal investigation, it is too late to undo the ripples or hide the corroborative evidence of your life. The investigating officers will be turning over the stones of your day-to-day existence to make their case for the District Attorney. They will talk to your neighbors, turn your house inside out, search and download the contents of your cell phone, obtain a search warrant for your financial records, your social media accounts and seize or photograph anything that they think refutes your claim of self-defense. For that reason, it is critical to act and live reasonably—by appearance and practice—long before you are in that life or death moment of choosing to shoot or die, to kill or be killed.

THE LAW OF SELF-DEFENSE
When members of the community are called to serve, and ultimately selected to sit as jurors in a criminal trial, they are provided instruction by the court, which explains their role in the trial process, the rules they must follow, and the obligations of the

125

respective parties in the case, if any. These instructions or assemblage of rules and practices are generally referred to by Court and Counsel as *Jury Instructions*. In my state, we rely on the California Criminal Jury Instructions which have been drafted and approved by the State Supreme Court, after drafts and amendments by a committee selected by that Court, for that purpose. This collection of rules is referred to in shorthand as "CALCRIM".

The CALCRIM instructions are a simplification of the most frequently addressed areas of law in criminal jury trials. They reflect substantive charges most often litigated in criminal jury trials, as well as the most common defenses employed, and address the peripheral issues of trials, such as which party proceeds first, who has the burden of proof, what needs to be proven and the rights of the parties in that venue.

Juries in homicide trials are given instruction on the definition of homicide and murder. They are instructed about legal concepts like *malice aforethought, implied malice* and the *specific intent to kill*. They are also instructed on the concept of *Heat of Passion,* which can permit a jury to determine that a defendant committed Voluntary Manslaughter rather than Murder. Juries are also instructed on Self-Defense as a legal concept in certain cases. They are informed that the District Attorney, in addition to proving the crime of Murder or Manslaughter must also prove beyond a reasonable doubt that the Defendant did not commit the act in Self-Defense or Defense of Others. This can be a formidable burden to the prosecution.

Most homicide cases deal with the intent or State of Mind of the Defendant at the critical moment they chose to engage in the act that is now the underpinning of the case before the jury. The entire case often times boils down to: why the person shot/stabbed/beat or otherwise injured or killed another person, what were they thinking, and whether their perception of the given threat was reasonable, or the result of a predisposition for violence.

Rarely is a jury given the benefit of direct evidence. Rarely does a defendant tell the investigating officers why he killed the decedent or injured the "victim." In cases where the Defendant does provide a statement of intent, or state of mind, law enforcement often times does not believe him or her, or sets out to disprove their claimed basis for acting. This investigation into motive is often the most critical component of many cases, and therefore where the attorneys spend most of their emphasis litigating the case.

CALCRIM 223

CALCRIM 223 advises the jury that the District Attorney and the Defense can establish facts in trial not only by Direct Evidence, but also by Circumstantial Evidence. They are advised as follows.

> Facts may be proved by direct or circumstantial evidence or by a combination of both. *Direct evidence* can prove a fact by itself. For example, if a witness testifies he saw it raining outside before he came into the courthouse, that testimony is direct evidence that it was raining. *Circumstantial evidence* also may be called indirect evidence. Circumstantial evidence does not directly prove the fact to be decided, but is evidence of another fact or group of facts from which you may conclude the truth of the fact in question. For example, if a witness testifies that he saw someone come inside wearing a raincoat covered with drops of water, that testimony is circumstantial evidence because it may support a conclusion that it was raining outside. Both direct and circumstantial evidence are acceptable types of evidence to prove or disprove the elements of a charge, including intent and mental state and acts necessary to a conviction, and neither is necessarily more reliable than the other. Neither is entitled to any greater weight than the other. You must decide whether a fact in issue has been proved based on all the evidence.

This singular instruction authorizes, legitimizes and sets the parameters for a thorough review of a Defendant's life because now, "Circumstantial Evidence" of your state of mind can be used by either party to prove their case. This instruction opens the door to a thorough review of how you lived your life up to the moment you pulled the trigger. CALCRIM 223 puts a Defendant's daily living under a microscope.

The Pandora's box of evidence that can be admitted as relevant evidence is immense. This evidence can be used by either party and considered by the Jury to convict or exonerate a person facing the most serious, critical and potentially devastating decision of a person's life; a decision made by complete and total strangers, many of whom may not share a Defendant's value system, life style, or familial or personal history and challenges.

CALCRIM 50

CALCRIM 50 sets forth the parameters of Self-Defense and Defense of Others in Homicide cases, which again, the prosecution must defeat. However, that instruction also provides a Defendant's attorney with the guidance and parameters for the admission of evidence that can demonstrate why you should go home rather than prison, even though you intentionally took someone's life. CALCRIM 505 Advises the Jury as follows.

JUSTIFIABLE HOMICIDE: SELF-DEFENSE OR DEFENSE OF ANOTHER

The defendant is not guilty of (murder/ [or] manslaughter/ attempted murder/ [or] attempted voluntary manslaughter) if (he/ she) was justified in (killing/attempting to kill) someone in (self-defense/ [or] defense of another). The defendant acted in lawful (self-defense/ [or] defense of another) if:

1. The defendant reasonably believed that (he/she/ [or] someone else/ [or] <insert name or description of third party>) was in imminent danger of being killed or suffering great bodily injury [or was in imminent danger of being (raped/maimed/robbed/ <insert other forcible and atrocious crime>)];

2. The defendant reasonably believed that the immediate use of deadly force was necessary to defend against that danger; AND

3. The defendant used no more force than was reasonably necessary to defend against that danger.

Belief in future harm is not sufficient, no matter how great or how likely the harm is believed to be. The defendant must have believed there was imminent danger of great bodily injury to (himself/herself/ [or] someone else). Defendant's belief must have been reasonable and (he/she) must have acted only because of that belief. The defendant is only entitled to use that amount of force that a reasonable person would believe is necessary in the same situation. If the defendant used more force than was reasonable, the [attempted] killing was not justified.

128

When deciding whether the defendant's beliefs were reasonable, consider all the circumstances as they were known to and appeared to the defendant and consider what a reasonable person in a similar situation with similar knowledge would have believed. If the defendant's beliefs were reasonable, the danger does not need to have actually existed. Therefore, the jury is advised that the District Attorney MUST PROVE BEYOND A REASONABLE DOUBT that you did not Reasonably Believe that you or someone else were in imminent danger of becoming the victim of a violent or atrocious crime, that the force or violence that your employed was unreasonable and that your perception of that threat was unreasonable. As you can see in the verbiage of the Jury Instruction the word REASONABLE is paramount to the jury's evaluation of your decision to shoot and/or kill.

It is common for a specific Jury Instruction to refer to other Jury Instructions to supplementally explain a concept or a word as it is employed in the context of a criminal jury trial. The word and concept of "Reasonableness" is one of the most critical in criminal law. Therefore "reasonable" has its own jury instruction. This is important because jurors often times disagree on what is and what is not reasonable.

In the context of self-defense, the jury will be provided the following definition to determine whether your perceptions, actions and use of force were reasonable.

Reasonable force

The amount of force that a **reasonable person** in the same situation would believe is **necessary** to neutralize the threat. When deciding whether the defendant used reasonable force, consider all the **circumstances** as they were **known to and appeared to the defendant** and consider what a reasonable person in a similar situation with similar knowledge would have believed. If the defendant's beliefs were reasonable, the danger does not need to have actually existed.

As you can see, the definition of reasonable is defined by referring to a *mythical reasonable person*. If this definition feels circuitous, your perception is not unique. Defining reasonableness is much like defining common sense—these definitions rely on each individual juror's filters. Those filters are greatly influenced by each juror's personal history, their

129

struggles and accomplishments, and their resulting opinions and values as to how a person should live their life and when they can fight back. Therefore, in the jury deliberation room, you literally have 12 potentially very different value systems and micro communities judging your lifestyle and decisions to determine if you are a reasonable person that they should believe made a justified or excusable decision.

In evaluating your decision, they will employ and contrast two main components: their own lives and your life. Their lives will be the foundation upon which they perceive a reasonable person. They will automatically revert to how they think they would have perceived a threat and what they think they would have done in response. This becomes difficult when the life experience of your juror is drastically different than yours. For some of my clients this means clean, organized and employed suburban jurors making judgment calls about the life, lifestyle and decisions employed by an 18-year-old gang member. For other clients, it means the same juror who might also be nonviolent, passive and scared of firearms making a judgment call about a 25 to 45-year-old Concealed Carry Licensee who took the life of another person in circumstances where law enforcement felt it was not justified or excusable.

These are circumstances where the value system of the juror(s) may not be aligned with those of the client. In those moments, which are frequent, it is imperative that the indirect evidence or corroborative evidence I spoke of above is positive, helpful or at a bare minimum, neutral.

CORROBORATIVE EVIDENCE OF A REASONABLE LIFE
When that critical moment arrives and you sit at counsel table in a packed courtroom and the attorneys begin to peel back the layers of your life in an effort to reveal who you are as an indication of why you pulled that trigger, it is critical that the evidence supports your affirmative self-defense or again, at a minimum doesn't undermine it.

The jury will be presented with evidence that demonstrates your value system: your core ideals that reveal who you are. Identifying your worst qualities as a human being, evidenced by the photographic, literary and digital trail that you leave behind in your everyday life—your "ripples", if you will.

They will identify and present prior acts of violence, road rage, spats with co-workers and strong political statements to demonstrate that you are an impetuous, strong willed person, hell bent and predisposed to be callous, reckless and/or violent. They will then argue that it is those traits that led you to pull the trigger and take a life, rather than a last second, last chance frightful and desperate decision to protect yourself or someone else from imminent death or great bodily injury at the hands of the decedent.

As I said when I opened the chapter, we leave ripples in our lives much like the stone breaking the water. These ripples are found in the way we dress, the way we spend money, the manner in which we interact with others and more importantly how we spend our time researching the world on our computers and phones and most importantly, how we put ourselves on display in social media.

FINANCIAL RECORDS

Money does NOT grow on trees. The vast majority of us have had to earn whatever small piece of the universe we have been able to attain by working long hours, committing to a career, and caring for our loved ones with the money that reflects our blood, sweat and sometimes tears. For that reason, when we spend money, it necessarily reflects a decision of what is important to us, over other priorities. When an adult with other obligations chooses to purchase a firearm or accessories, or upgrade that weapon, it reflects a balance of hours of our lives lost, and precedence to that expense. For this reason, your purchase, upgrade or modification of a firearm may be made an important factor in the microscopic evaluation of your life and mindset. Some folks modify their weapon, which is not necessarily a negative decision, but I caution you to modify it in a manner that appears reasonable to someone who may be scrutinizing your life when you least want them to. For example, if you are considering engraving your weapon with a logo or a phrase, reflect for a moment on how that modification might look to another person if that weapon is thereafter on an evidence table in a homicide trial. When a cash-strapped juror who is not a huge fan of guns, sees the "Smile. Wait for Flash" engraving on the muzzle of your tricked out, modified 1911, will it be more difficult to argue that you had no choice other than to take a life? Probably.

If you take the time and money to engrave a biblical phrase or a military phrase upon your firearm, it represents time and money committed to a state of mind that might be considered braggadocios, callous, arrogant or "unreasonable".

131

Therefore, I strongly recommend that you NOT engrave your weapon and if you do modify it, that you stop and think for a minute how that modification might be perceived by a single mother of three who believes in protecting children, but not in the right to be a bully, or take a life recklessly.

CLOTHING

Much like money spent on a weapon or subsequent modification thereof, money spent on clothing and our manner of dress reveals a lot about how we perceive the world, ourselves and how we want to be perceived by others. Silk-screened shirts have been around for decades and have a variety of images, sayings, phrases and themes. Sci-Fi geeks choose Star Wars and Star Trek shirts. Liberals choose shirts demonizing their conservative opponents. Conservatives wear shirts and hats poking fun at the liberal left.

Many of us hold overt or even subtle political viewpoints and when we find stickers, shirts or hats that corroborate those views, or mock the opposing argument, we elect to pay for and wear those clothes in an effort to entertain, offend or at least let others know how we feel. The problem is that many messages, images and even symbols can imply callousness about the opposing point of view. In the realm of firearms, and the hotly debated discussion surrounding the Second Amendment, Gun Control and whether firearms are the source of violence or merely a tool sometimes selected by the otherwise criminally minded individuals, a strongly displayed message or point of view can offend other people, or appear arrogant. One of those people might be a juror who is making a very critical decision about how you spend the remainder of your life.

If you have shirts in your wardrobe that mock the gun control lobby, or their enthusiasts, and worse, if you're wearing one of them at that critical moment when you discharge your weapon, you are giving the District Attorney corroborative evidence to argue that you are not a reasonable person. For instance, with all facts being the same, if I represent a client that is wearing a nice polo shirt or button down shirt versus a t-shirt that is emblazoned "Kill 'em All. Let God sort them out", the first client is going to have a much better chance at arguing self-defense before the same jury. If you are arrested for a homicide in your residence, you can rest assured that the officers will obtain a warrant to search your home. If your closet or dresser is filled with rhetoric that is pro-gun, anti gun-control, and espousing your right to defend yourself or worse, rid society of ne'er do wells, the clothes will be seized or at least photographed and shown to the jury in an effort to argue that you are NOT in fact a reasonable person who had to take a life, but rather an armed crusader who finally got their chance to kill someone they consider to be less than human.

I recommend that you dress reasonably. Wear non-descript clothing that doesn't advertise your political views. Even if that view isn't related to firearms, you may trigger an unwanted reaction from someone who opposes your politics and in this very divided society, end up in an altercation. If your politically oriented clothing is the source of the underlying argument that triggered the shooting, you can rest assured that the prosecutor will be arguing that you are not a level headed victim who barely escaped with their life, but rather an antagonist who was looking for trouble and found it. Your clothing can literally condemn you to prison if you are not careful.

DEMEANOR

Your demeanor at the moment of the incident and the moments immediately before and after will also be under scrutiny. Your best scenario is to be described as calm and happy when suddenly confronted by an attacker whom you had no choice other than to neutralize. If there are descriptions by witnesses of you engaging in antagonistic behavior immediately before the incident with other people, before your ultimate confrontation with the decedent, the District Attorney is again going to paint you as an aggravated bully or at a minimum, someone who was looking for trouble and acted on it when you interacted with the decedent.

When you call 911, your call will be recorded. This phone call can be critical. It reflects your initial statement of events, but also records so much more. If you are antagonistic, angry, arrogant, cocky, remorseful, scared, sad and pleading for the quick response of law enforcement, it will give the jury what they perceive as a critical insight into your soul and a valuable gauge of your reasonableness.

If you are forced to call 911, please remember to be calm, clear and seeking the assistance of law enforcement. Stay on the phone with dispatch and be sure to convey your fear, not your anger. Let the dispatcher know you are armed and if the suspect is known, their identity. Remember that the call is recorded and if possible, before pulling the trigger advise the decedent that you are armed, and on the phone with police. This alone may keep you from having to shoot, but it also lets the jury hear three years later in that jury trial, the efforts you made to avoid that ultimate conflict. It lets them hear you pleading for help and your tearful demeanor.

Try to avoid anger and rage in that moment. Anger is always a second emotion. Try to remain in your primary emotion, which is most likely fear and convey that. If, you threaten the decedent, we can explain it at trial, but it is another layer that we must work through. Therefore, if you let them know you are armed, please tell the intruder that you are armed and will shoot "if I have to." This gives the intruder the option to leave and lets the dispatcher and subsequent jury know that you didn't want to shoot and only did so because it was necessary.

When officers arrive, remain tearful and in your primary emotion. If you transition to anger or rage, it will make your subsequent trial more complicated. Understand that you will be detained and most likely handcuffed. You may hold officers in very high esteem and have family members and friends who are cops, but the officers who respond that night will likely not know you and will want to make sure all threats are neutralized before they start asking questions.

Do not become angry or defensive if the officers appear rude, indifferent or even abrasive upon their arrival. Comply with their directives, understanding that they need to secure the scene before they can figure out what happened. Don't argue or become defensive. Most officers these days have body cameras and your demeanor will again be on display for a jury at a later date.

SOCIAL MEDIA / PHONE CONTENT / COMPUTERS
Probably the single most important source of corroborative information on reasonableness is Social Media and how we use our computers and phones. What we search for, which pictures we take and keep and most importantly, how we reveal and display ourselves on social media can reveal a lot about our personalities. If your social media feed is filled with photos of your family, well wishes and charitable events, you will have a much easier time arguing you are a reasonable person, than if you fill those mediums with mocking comments about the gun control lobby, intellectually challenged liberals and threads

134

about what is wrong with society and how you could repair it if you had the chance.

Homicide detectives are tireless in their efforts to find evidence. Facebook, Instagram and other social media apps have special divisions set up for handling warrant requests for data because it is such a common practice. So, if your Facebook feed has rants about predators, burglars or the anti-gun lobby, they will be revealed in the response to a search warrant. The District Attorney will seek to admit those posts or comments in an effort to demonstrate a predisposition toward firearm violence, which undermines your attorney's argument at trial that you are a reasonable person who had no choice other than to pull that trigger. I strongly encourage you to moderate your social media activity, recognizing that it could be used against you at the very moment that it can hurt you the most. Realize that not everyone may agree with your political points of view, and if you are being judged by a jury of 12 more than one of them may not be impressed by your wit, humor or point of view and hold it against you in determining whether you should go to prison or go home.

The same is true for the contents of your cell phone. Search warrants for cell phones are common. If you have videos or photos of yourself shooting an illegal rifle, or shooting a photograph of a former liberal president or any other demonstration of sarcasm or political activism with a gun it will be shown to the jury.

Finally, if your search history is obtained and you have sought information on how to kill a burglar and get away with it, or the best way to appear sympathetic in front of a jury, that conduct alone could have a huge impact on your case. Research of weapons, or politics or any other topic, which might be misunderstood or used against you, should be done with an incognito tab so that the history of that search is not preserved and cannot be used against you.

RESIDENTIAL DECORE

Much like all other aspects of our lives discussed above, the way we decorate our homes can say a lot about us. Much like your social media feed, if your walls are adorned with photos of your children and family events, you have a much better chance of being portrayed as a reasonable person than if your walls are covered in pro gun slogans.

If you have a sign by your front door that indicates trespassers will be shot, we might be able to argue that you're simply giving notice to potential intruders. If the second line of the same sign indicates that survivors will be shot again, our job will be more difficult. Signs or posters indicating that your house is protected by Smith and Wesson or that moments of silence indicate you are loading or reloading your gun, the signs will likely be seized or at a minimum be photographed and shown to the jury in the fight between your counsel and the prosecutor over whether you are a person they should find to be reasonable. Therefore, I recommend you consider how you decorate your house, your room, your den and even your garage. These signs, posters and neon lights can say a lot about you in the eyes of a stranger who may be making the most important decision in your life. You will substantially increase your chances of a successful analysis of that critical question if you decorate your house in a manner that is neutral and family oriented.

CLOSING

Having prosecuted and defended thousands of bad decisions over the past quarter-century, I've dealt with virtually every bad decision a human being can make. These decisions can range from opting to drive after a few drinks because a person feels fine to drive, all the way to the ultimate decision, to take the life of another human being. Many decisions that land a person in criminal court are irreversible in the sense that the aftermath, or ripples of that underlying decision leave an indelible mark on a person's life and often, the lives of others. This is no truer than where one person kills another.

Killing someone triggers enormous potential liability that can include the loss of: your job, your spouse, your family, your assets, reputation, and more importantly the loss of your freedom, and in some very limited circumstance, the loss of your life. Making the decision to carry a firearm and following through with the necessary training, time and effort to select a firearm to carry, accessories and the day-to-day challenge to remain concealed and safe requires a deliberate act. It is a tremendous commitment.

Realizing that your decision to pull that trigger can put everything at risk, take a moment to evaluate your life objectively. Review your social media feed, look through your wardrobe and evaluate whether you're behaving in a manner that is giving you the best chance to look like a reasonable person when the State starts turning over rocks in your life.

In essence, live your life reasonably. Appear reasonable. Carry yourself as a reasonable person. Be humble and adorn your body and house in a manner that demonstrates a humble and reasonable state of mind. These small things can make all the difference when you are under a microscope in a courtroom with everything you hold dear at risk.

A NOTE ON THE AUTHOR

Michael Wise is the principal attorney of the Wise Law Group, PC in Sacramento, California and focuses his practice on criminal defense of clients ranging from simple matters like DUI, up to complex allegations such as felony assault, narcotics, domestic violence, fraud and homicide. He has achieved acquittals for clients on multiple cases, including domestic violence, assault and murder. A former prosecutor, Mr. Wise has earned a reputation as a tenacious litigator who is well respected by colleagues, judges and even law enforcement. He frequently teaches law enforcement officers about the tenets of criminal investigation, report writing and testimony in court. Mr. Wise has prosecuted and/or defended virtually every category of criminal conduct.

A fervent advocate for the Second Amendment, Mr. Wise also frequently speaks to Concealed Weapons Permit applicants at DefenseSHOT about the privileges and risks of carrying a loaded firearm. He educates students on the law of self-defense in California, and more importantly, the potential interpretation and scrutiny of their lifestyle before a critical incident, as well as their behavior immediately before, during and after a shooting occurs. By instructing students about how their lives and choices may be dissected and presented to a jury, Mr. Wise hopes to help CCW Licensees be better suited to defend themselves if they are charged criminally or civilly if it becomes necessary to shoot another person.

Contributed by Michael Wise. Copyright © Kendall Hunt Publishing Company.

— Chapter 17 —

GUT INSTINCT
By John Daniels Sr.

John Daniels 1965

WITH 35+ YEARS IN LAW-ENFORCEMENT, one of the most important tools I've learned to use is that of paying attention to your feelings. Some call it a sixth sense, intuition, or hunch. We all have the ability to take advantage of it, but often ignore it or let it pass, not acting on the hunch. All of us should be aware of our surroundings and be sensitive to this natural input of information. Many times—almost daily—I benefit from the value of this gift. Walking, driving, interacting with others gives you the opportunity to experience this. Over the years, I have made many, many arrests, avoided accidents, located missing persons, and saved lives (including my own) based on a hunch or a feeling. Often there is no obvious reason based in fact, or string of events that lead you to such a feeling. Something in your subconscious speaks to you, and warns or directs your next move or action. Being a man of faith, I attribute this to God, and believe everything happens for a reason-good or bad. We may never know why things occur the way they do. If something just doesn't feel right, if you sense danger, or see something out of place, pay attention to it. It may require action on your part to avoid an unfavorable outcome. The following are a dozen of the many cases where this "sixth sense" made a difference.

ONE SUMMER NIGHT
One summer night, I was patrolling and checking back alleyways in the business district of the city of Stanton in southern California. When I came to the end of an alley, I stopped and looked across the street near the corner of Main Street just off Beach Blvd. at the Tick Tock Market. I had been cruising stealthily through the ally with my lights "blacked out" by activating a switch on the dashboard that disables all the patrol car lights including the brake lights. I noticed a red Mustang convertible with the top down, containing two adult males, circle the market and park at the closed gas station next to the market. The reason this stood out was the fact that there were no cars parked at the market at that time, so there was plenty of parking available. My inner voice told me to call for backup and I directed the second unit to come up the alley the same way I had with lights blacked out. The two male occupants of the Mustang exited the car. They walked over and entered the market. My backup unit arrived and together we observed.

Both men pulled semi-automatic handguns; they ordered a clerk—a male about age thirty—to the back of the store. The suspects emptied the cash register and filled paper bags full of cigarette cartons before walking out. Not wanting the incident to turn into a hostage situation, we waited for the suspects to exit the store and put some distance between them and the front door. When they walked halfway between the store and their vehicle, we crossed the street and took them by surprise with their hands full. Each one of them was carrying two full paper bags in their arms. The clerk was located in the back cooler and was unharmed. It was later at the Police Department while writing my report next to the holding cell that I overheard one of the suspects tell the other that they needed a good attorney. The second suspect answered, "When two cops sit across the street and watch you hold a place up you plead guilty." While checking the vehicle out after securing both suspects, I noticed what appeared to be a couple of bullet holes in the rear trunk lid. It turned out that these two suspects had held up a gun store in Los Angeles and were involved in a shoot out with the store owner while fleeing another previous hold up were they had successfully gained cash and guns. Ultimately, they were tried and convicted after I testified in L.A. and they were put away for years. We were treated like royalty for catching them. I seemed to fall into something major every couple weeks to the point that other cops were calling me "Adam 12", but I'm just giving you a few examples here.

Another incident occurred one summer night around 11pm when I was patrolling to the rear of some apartments in Stanton. I noticed a motorcycle – a silver and black Honda Scrambler - parked near the perimeter fence. *A feeling* told me this was suspicious as there was plenty of parking near the apartments. I waited a moment a short distance away until the subject—a white, clean cut male in his early twenties in jeans and a blue T-shirt approached the bike. I pulled up and engage the suspect requesting his driver's license and registration to positively identify him as the owner of the motorcycle. I also felt the side of the motor and noted it was still warm and hadn't been there long. While I was asking him questions, the radio dispatcher advised me of a rape report in the same apartments and the dispatcher gave me the suspect's description as I stood there looking at my suspect. I noticed the subject I was questioning fit it to a tee, and I placed him under arrest. The victim came out to the parking lot and positively identified the suspect. He had broken into her apartment while she was showering and grabbed her as she was walking down the hall wrapped in a towel. This was a stranger rape and there was no connection between the victim and suspect. If I hadn't paid attention to that still small voice, he would have gotten away with it.

There was a time one summer night when one of our deputies was missing under suspicious circumstances and maybe suicidal. He was known to be driving a four-wheel drive Jeep soft-top. I knew he was familiar with the back roads of the Camino and Pollock Pines area. As I searched various back roads and out-of-the-way places, I checked the area of Rock Creek Reservoir Damn. I drove up the narrow dirt road on the south side of the damn to a small area where a few people sometimes launch small boats. *I had this feeling* as I looked into the water, even though I didn't see bubbles or an oil slick. I was thinking that this officer could have seat belted himself in and shot himself allowing his Jeep to roll into the water and be submerged. The divers recovered him secured inside his vehicle at that location. He was a good officer and friend, but had a lot of personal issues that he felt he could not deal with. Again that still quiet voice guided me and I didn't hesitate to follow it; as horrific as the outcome was, at least the family members didn't have to continue with uncertainty.

On another occasion one summer, I was the detective investigating a burglary and safe job at the Sierra Nevada House, a very active restaurant and bar in Coloma. I had a possible suspect, a man in his early thirties who was on probation and lived in the area in a trailer at Camp Coloma. I brought him to the Sheriff's Department for questioning, but could not link him to the case or break his alibi. *I had this feeling* that he was the suspect, but was running out of questions and had no evidence on which to hold him. I left the interview room and went to my desk, which sat across from the interview room door. I opened my desk drawer and took out some old latent print cards from an older, unrelated case. It should be noted that while processing this Sierra Nevada House crime scene, I was unable to lift any latent prints off the safe, due to its crinkle paint surface. I returned to the interview room and tossed the old print cards on the table in front of the suspect. I then asked him if he could explain how his prints got on the safe. He admitted to the burglary and safe job on tape. He signed a confession statement and was subsequently sent to prison for many years.

On another occasion one summer night while serving a search warrant and trying to locate a rape suspect at the Virginia Thomas apartments next to Camino Lumber, I was checking the bathroom shower and noticed a large pile of dirty clothes in the stall. *I had a feeling* that something wasn't right, and in fact it might be possible for someone to hide under the clothes. As I peeled back a few items of clothing, I noticed an ear. I put the muzzle of my 357 Magnum to the exposed ear, and ordered the suspect out. He was taken into custody without further incident. After this suspect did his time, he was released only later to kill his brother and return to prison.

In some cases, victims either neglect to listen to their gut instinct, or had no notion of how to best respond when put into a dangerous spot. I had a case one summer where two women in there thirties were walking during their lunch break at the welfare office. A man in a car pulled up and ordered them into the car at gunpoint. He took them to a secluded spot, attacked them and ended up leaving them both for dead after crushing their heads with a rock. One survived. She regained consciousness and crawled to the road for help. I was the lead detective investigating the case. The suspect was apprehended and is in prison. Everyone should be told that if anyone orders you into a vehicle, yell and run. Your chances of survival are a lot better. Usually the suspect is going to flee the area with no shots fired. Let this sink into your subconscious. When you hear that small voice inside your head, or gut, telling you something, listen and act accordingly. It could save your life, and the lives of others. It can also often times keep you out of trouble in the first place.

ONE WINTER NIGHT

One winter night I was dispatched to a residential fire on Cottage Street in Placerville, Ca. Upon arrival, I observed the firemen attempting to hose down the heavily involved house resulting from a chimney fire. *I had a feeling*. So I inquired about possible residents inside and if the house had been cleared. The fireman stated that a neighbor advised them that no one was home and that they were out of town. I insisted that they enter the structure and check. As it turned out, the man was out of town but his wife and two young children were still inside. The smoke had them disorientated and they would not have escaped without being rescued. They were later cleared at the hospital without injury other than smoke inhalation.

One winter day in heavy rain, I was investigating a despondent missing persons report off Mosquito Road near Swansboro. After talking with the missing child's mother, I began driving and conducting a search of the general area. Suddenly, as I was driving, *I got this feeling* at one specific curve in the road. I stopped and exited the vehicle. I walked a short distance and looked down a steep embankment where I observed the missing teenage girl sitting on the limb of a large oak tree that protruded out of the side of the hill, overhanging another steep embankment. She was approximately 60 to 80 feet above the ground on that side of the tree. I proceeded to climb down to the base of the tree and noted a white nylon rope around her neck with the other end tied to the huge tree limb she was sitting on. I climbed out onto the tree just below her location, and began a conversation with her about life and how much more she had to experience, what she would miss out on, how this would effect her loved ones, etc. We were in that tree in the pouring winter rain for a couple of hours or more. I was so soaked, even my bulletproof vest was soaked through. I was even becoming hypothermic. It's a wonder I didn't fall out of the tree. At one point, I advised her that if she did jump, or fall, that I would just shoot the rope with my handgun as she fell. I told here she would just end up breaking some bones and being in a lot of pain, so she may as well untie the rope and come down out of the tree, which she ultimately did. Unless I made the perfect shot -which was highly unlikely even with my shooting ability- as she jumped and before the rope went taught, she would have succeeded in breaking her neck, but I kept that to myself. She was taken for psychological help and is still with us today, decades later.

ONCE I IGNORED THE STILL SOFT VOICE

A time I regret not acting on a feeling that occurred while on motorcycle patrol. I noticed a blue Chevy Nova pull out of an alleyway and head north on Beach Blvd. in a rushed manner. Something didn't feel right, but I couldn't put my finger on it and I let it slide. This happened during the day in heavy traffic and I have no idea why that particular vehicle stood out to me at the time, or why *I had an unusual feeling* about it. It turned out later, it was a suspect vehicle involved in a kidnapping where a young teenage female was kidnapped by a man near a Carl's Jr. on Beach Blvd. Fortunately, the vehicle was stopped approximately 300 miles away en route to the Bay Area, and the suspect was taken into custody with the victim unharmed, for which I am grateful. I would hate to have that on my conscience.

One day my detective partner and I were working on a case together when we copied on the radio, a large pursuit was eastbound on Highway 50 with a bank hold up suspect. *I had a feeling* that the suspect might take the El Dorado Road off-ramp to avoid downtown Placerville traffic. I pulled our unmarked unit (an unusual tan, turbo charged late model Mustang that had been seized in a drug bust, and then converted for law enforcement use) to the side of the road at the end of the off-ramp. My partner and I exited the vehicle, and took up positions at the end of the ramp. This pursuit started in Sacramento, and the bank robbery suspect was armed and driving a stolen vehicle, a brand new full-size sedan he was test-driving from a new car lot. The suspect came up the freeway with a long parade of marked and unmarked units in tow lights and sirens blaring. He stayed in the fast lane until it looked like he would pass the off-ramp. Sure enough, at the last second the suspect swerved hard and took the East-bound El Dorado Road off-ramp. As he raced up the ramp, we stepped out with guns drawn. He ended up stopping right in front of us and gave up. The pursuing units pulled up and took him into custody. While debriefing, my partner mentioned he had been aiming at the tire. I was aiming at the driver since he was driving right at us.

John
Daniels
1984

On another occasion, I was briefed prior to my patrol shift about a kidnapping suspect in a vehicle. I was advised that a female adult that was being transported in a mental health van had somehow got behind the wheel and left the area with another subject inside. The passenger was later let out and the van was possibly headed for the Georgetown area via Highway 193 north of Placerville, California. While patrolling the area of

Georgetown, and later Swansboro, *I had a feeling* about an isolated area near Finnon Reservoir. I had not been out this dirt trail before. The trail led off from a parking area on dirt and gravel where logging trucks would park from time to time. Why I drove out this trail I don't know, except something told me to do so. After driving approximately half a mile, I observed the back of a white van. I parked my patrol car a short distance away, advised dispatch, and walked toward the van. Just prior to getting to the van, a female adult emerged from the brush and started walking toward me. As I started to engage her in conversation, she bent down and picked up a beer bottle holding it by the neck and pulling her arm back to use the bottle as a weapon. I talked to her in a calm manner, and reasoned with her about the escalating charges of assaulting an officer and resisting arrest. I told her that I would help her if I could, and put in a good word with the court. She dropped the bottle and submitted to arrest without further incident. On the way to jail, via Rock Creek Road, the suspect slipped her handcuffed arms from her back under her legs to the front. She tried to persuade me to pull off on a side road to engage in sex with her – obviously this would have been to gain an opportunity to attack me and escape. She pulled up her top exposing her breasts. When I told her I was not interested she became enraged and started pulling all the foam padding off the cage separation in the unit. I advised dispatch that I would need assistance upon arrival, and expedited my travel time so the suspect could not accuse me of taking advantage of her.

On another occasion, my partner and I we're serving a search warrant on a cabin in the fresh pond area of the Sierra Mountains near Lake Tahoe. A bank robbery suspect was renting the house. The bank robbery had occurred in Nevada. We were conducting a search of the house after taking the suspect into custody along with his accomplice girlfriend who, oddly enough was proud of her profession as a prostitute at the Mustang Ranch in Nevada. She insisted that we list her occupation as such on her booking paperwork. I was in the process of searching under the kitchen sink in the cabin, and observed a rolled up burlap bag. I removed the bag from under the sink and sat it on the floor. My partner said, "What's in that?" and started to kick at the bag. As he swung his foot at the bag, I caught his foot and cautioned him not to kick it because we had no idea what was in the bag. *I had a feeling* about the bag. It turned out, the bag contained seven sticks of dynamite that had already started leaking nitroglycerine droplets on their surface, and the droplets of nitro had crystallized, making the dynamite very unstable and very dangerous. Kicking the bag could have caused an explosion that would have leveled the cabin and killed us. All the dynamite was too dangerous to be transported and thus, had to be burned onsite by the bomb disposal unit.

These are only just a few of the incidents where the sixth sense or being guided by that still small voice paid off over my career.

Pay attention to your feelings. It might save your life and those around you. Be aware of your surroundings and look ahead to anticipate potential problems. Don't be paranoid about it, but consider possible scenarios that might come up in various situations that you're in. Consider the area you're in, and try to think what a bad person might do utilizing the possible cover in the area. Stay alert and off your cellphone when out in public. Remember there is relative safety in numbers. Always let people know where you're going and when you expect to return.

Contributed by John W. Daniels. Copyright © Kendall Hunt Publishing Company.
All photos courtesy of Linda Daniels.

EL DORADO
COUNTY
COURT HOUSE

John Daniels
Early 2000's

— Chapter 18 —

NO WEAPON FORMED AGAINST YOU WILL PROSPER

SOMETIMES I'LL HEAR PEOPLE SAY THINGS LIKE, "I don't need a gun or a CCW license because God will take care of me." I know for a fact the same people have a driver's license. Hopefully, they're looking both ways before pulling out into traffic. Obviously, the logic that is applied for "God taking care of you" seems to have strange and illogical dividing lines. Please understand, this is actually a fringe idea. As a Christian myself, I do not subscribe to the above. The pastors and clergy I have trained over the years also agree—there's nothing wrong with carrying a gun. It is not a result of "weak faith in God." Weak faith (according to the Bible) is something entirely different.

Weak faith means a Christian who unfortunately still believes God is judging him by how well he follows the Ten Commandments and 600 plus other rules known as "The law" after he has been saved. Galatians 5:4 says, "Christ is become of no effect unto you, whosoever of you are justified by the law; ye are fallen from grace." That, according to the Bible, is weak faith. "Falling from grace" is clearly not a good thing.

Faith, as it applies to God, has nothing to do with blindly crossing the road without looking. Instead, faith is realizing that Jesus is God, (John1 and many other places); that he came here and lived a perfect and sinless life and that he made you right with Him by dying in your place, having taken responsibility for the myriad sins we have committed, and those we will commit. Once we accept his payment, made on our behalf, He gives us credit for living the perfect life that Jesus lived. As a result, you are *saved* and permanently right with God. Not by your actions and deeds (because earning perfection is impossible), but instead by accepting His gift on your behalf. Faith means you believe God sees you as if you are as perfect as Jesus Christ himself, because you accepted that gift. As a result, God will never, ever judge you negatively, because your debt was paid for at the cross. The Bible reiterates this time and again. John 3:18 lays it out succinctly. Everyone seems to know John 3:16, but few follow John's thought in context through to verse 18. So here we go. Pay attention to verses 17 and 18 this time.

John 3:16-18 (KJV):

16 For God so loved the world, that he gave his only begotten Son, that whosoever believeth in him should not perish, but have everlasting life. 17 For God sent not his Son into the world to condemn the world, but that the world through him might be saved. 18 He that believeth on him is not condemned: but he that believeth not is condemned already, because he hath not believed in the name of the only begotten Son of God.

Did you catch that? Faith is believing in Jesus (Jesus is God – John 1 and many other places in scripture), and you are forever accepted by God because you have accepted His gift. Have you accepted His gift for you? If you have, you are no longer judged by your actions or deeds and nothing will ever separate you from God. Now you can live, not motivated by judgment, but instead because you are happy about what He has done for you and the freedom of no longer being judged.

Next, I invite you to a challenge. For those who accept it's premise, this will be the sweetest fragrance you have ever enjoyed. For those who reject it, it will smell of death. Are you up to the challenge? To accept this challenge, send me an email at insructor@defenseshot.com with the word CHALLENGE in the subject line, and it will arrive promptly in your inbox.